A FUNDAMENTAL GOAL

A Fundamental Goal: Education for the People of Illinois

JANE GALLOWAY BURESH

Published for the
INSTITUTE OF GOVERNMENT AND PUBLIC AFFAIRS
by the
UNIVERSITY OF ILLINOIS PRESS
Urbana   Chicago   London

*Special appreciation is expressed to
the Field Foundation of Illinois,
whose financial support has made
this series possible.*

Library of Congress Cataloging in Publication Data

Buresh, Jane Galloway, 1945–
    A fundamental goal: education for the people
of Illinois.

    (Studies in Illinois constitution making)
    Originally presented as the author's thesis,
University of Chicago.
    1. Educational law and legislation — Illinois.
2. Illinois — Constitutional law. I. Illinois.
University at Urbana-Champaign. Institute of Govern-
ment and Public Affairs. II. Title. III. Series.
KFI1590.B87   1974   344'.773'07   74-19064
ISBN 0-252-00457-4 (pbk.)

To Jack

Contents

Foreword

When the Sixth Illinois Constitutional Convention convened in December 1969, many educational and political observers thought the question of state aid to private and parochial schools would be among the most difficult questions to resolve; some anticipated it would lead to a breakdown of the convention. Delegates campaigned on both sides of the issue, newspapers editorialized, interest groups took positions, and committee appointments in the convention were sought with that one question in mind. Surprisingly, the issue was resolved with little or no controversy. Both sides opted for the status quo — both sought to leave the constitutional language as it was in the 1870 document and allow the contestants to settle their battle in the courts.

But education was not without controversy in the convention. As Jane Buresh underscores in this volume, attention became focused on the questions of the priority of education as a state function, and the best means of carrying out that function. Neither issue received significant attention prior to the convention, nor was it immediately considered when the delegates were in the organization phase of their task. However, once the Education Committee began its work, and since the adjournment of the convention, the questions have taken on a new dimension. The way in which the participants in the Illinois political process address these two issues in the formative post-convention years will have profound impact on Illinois education for many years to come.

Ms. Buresh has analyzed the development of the legal and political framework for Illinois education. She has also laid a solid foundation for the continuing debate on the political questions related to education in Illinois, such as the role of state government in financing education and the relationship of the new state board of education to the established local boards.

A Fundamental Goal is the seventh volume in the series Studies in Illinois Constitution Making. The series was initiated as a result of a felt need for a thorough study of a state constitutional convention. Its primary aim is to recount — in breadth and detail — the events, personalities, strategies, conflicts, and resolutions which went into a new basic law acceptable to the voters of Illinois. Each book in the series deals with a specific phase of the convention utilizing an approach and method chosen by the author. Ms. Buresh, like the other authors, has combined her skill and background with first-hand observation of the convention and contact with the delegates. Ms. Buresh served as an administrative assistant to the Education Committee, and shared in much of the writing of the education article.

Publication of Studies in Illinois Constitution Making has been made possible by the generous support of the Field Foundation of Illinois. The statements and views expressed in these books are solely the responsibility of the authors.

JOSEPH P. PISCIOTTE
Series Editor

SAMUEL K. GOVE
Institute Director

Preface

The subject of education, as it relates to the Illinois Constitution, received very little attention from the press or from legal commentators either prior to or during the convention; relatively little time was devoted to debate on educational issues. And yet, it may be that the education article, of all the articles rewritten in 1970, will promote the most far-reaching changes — in financing, in scope, in the very nature of education as we know it today.

I was privileged to serve as the administrative assistant to the Education Committee at Illinois's Sixth Constitutional Convention. Thus, I was being paid a salary while at the same time I was doing research for a dissertation on the convention. What a happy situation for an impecunious graduate student! (Happier still because of the people with whom I worked at the convention.) My position as administrative assistant facilitated my observation of all but the earliest meetings of the committee, as well as the plenary sessions where the education article was considered.

Much of the information contained in this study is based on interviews with the delegates. The majority of these interviews were informal; I simply asked questions on specific issues. At other times, particularly with non–Education Committee members, I conducted interviews at length on the whole subject of education at the convention. In April 1970, I gave the Education Committee members a questionnaire which asked for their backgrounds, their answers to specific questions (such as, Who were the influential witnesses and lobbyists?), their positions on various educational issues prior to the convention, and an account of any changes in those positions after the convention began.

Other sources I consulted were the transcripts of the plenary sessions, member proposals, and the Education Committee minutes and reports; position papers of witnesses; mail received by the delegates; and records of previous constitutional conventions. After the convention ended, I accumulated missing information through correspondence with delegates, convention officials, and the Illinois Historical Library. Statistical data were supplied by the Illinois Education Association, the Office of the Superintendent of Public Instruction of Illinois, and the Board of Higher Education.

Acknowledgments are commonplace in a preface, but they are not sufficient to express my gratitude to all those who made this study possible. I wish to thank the delegates to the convention, most particularly the members of the Education Committee. I hope the following pages have adequately portrayed the dedication and the abilities of these eleven men and women. They kindly made me privy to information not usually accessible and thus permitted insight into their motivations — a subject always difficult to explore. Warm thanks also go to my special friends in the press corps covering the convention: Edie Herman of the *Chicago Tribune*, Charlie Wheeler of the *Chicago Sun-Times*, Ed Gilbreth and John Camper of the *Chicago Daily News* and Tony Abel of WCIA-TV in Champaign. Conversations with them added to my knowledge of the convention in general as well as to my enjoyment of the convention experience.

Members of the faculty and staff of the Institute of Government and Public Affairs of the University of Illinois could not have been more helpful: Samuel K. Gove, director; Ashley Nugent, technical advisor; and Jean Baker and Florence Edmison, typists. Thanks are due especially to Joseph Pisciotte, editor of this series, whose good humor and incisive insights kept me from depression and error; to Jane Clark, manuscript editor; and to the Field Foundation of Illinois which made this series possible.

This study was originally written as a Ph.D. dissertation for the University of Chicago. My greatest debt is to my dissertation committee: Philip B. Kurland, Donald A. Erickson, and especially my chairman, Robert L. McCaul. I am also grateful for the assistance of Dr. Richard G. Browne and Samuel W. Witwer, who were kind enough to read the manuscript before publication and to supplement my story with their own knowledge of the writing of the education article.

As administrative assistant to the Education Committee, I became totally immersed in the problems and personalities of the committee and the convention. I am sure that I was not a completely unbiased observer, and I am aware that my inclinations may often be apparent. Any errors in interpretation are solely my own.

Introduction

The Sixth Illinois Constitutional Convention was unique in Illinois constitutional history in several respects, all of which contributed to its success.

In the first place, no earlier convention had had the benefit of such extensive preparation to facilitate its task. More than four years before the convention formally opened in 1969, the Illinois General Assembly created the first of three successive constitution study commissions to engage in the crucial advance planning needed for the convention's work. Out of the efforts of these commissions came two very useful publications: George Braden and Rubin Cohn's *The Illinois Constitution: An Annotated and Comparative Analysis* and Thomas Kitsos and Joseph Pisciotte's *A Guide to Illinois Constitutional Revision: The 1969 Constitutional Convention,* both published by the Institute of Government and Public Affairs at the University of Illinois.

Another volume which proved invaluable to the delegates was prepared at the instigation of Governor Richard B. Ogilvie; it was a compilation of research by various scholars on potential issues for the convention and was called *Con-Con: Issues for the Illinois Constitutional Convention,* edited by Samuel K. Gove and Victoria Ranney and published by the University of Illinois Press. Various independent organizations also prepared research and position papers dealing with constitutional issues, many of which — according to observers at the convention — received extensive use by the delegates.

In the second place there had been for more than fifty years' concerted effort for constitutional revision. Every governor during that period had advocated extensive constitutional change by convention action or by separate amendment. These efforts, frequently frustrated by circumstances, had helped generate an unusual degree of public interest and support for the convention's work. Every major public official of the state was on record in support of the convention and all of them offered it their cordial assistance.

But the most unique feature of the Sixth Illinois Constitutional Convention was the quality of its 116 delegates. Senator W. Russell Arrington, addressing the convention on March 25, 1970, described them in these words:

> You are the most diverse and the best educated representative body ever assembled in this state. You are younger and more urban than any of the other five bodies that preceded you. Lawyers, educators, clergymen, government workers, business men, bankers, farmers, housewives, civil rights leaders — you are an impressive body.

From the outset, the delegates showed a deep commitment, a considerable exuberance, and a sense of destiny that set them apart. Their spirit was good from the start and their morale was lifted even higher when, on March 20, 1970, their deliberations moved into the beautifully restored, historic Old State Capitol.

This morale was steadily demonstrated by the pride the members took in their task — and in each other. Ms. Buresh has noted, with perception, the division of the Education Committee into "Young Turks" and "Old Guard"; but this factionalism, and even the gamesmanship it engendered, in no way disturbed the essential sense of unity among the members. They worked together, played together, and generally respected each other. They spoke admiringly of Catholic delegates who voted against any weakening of the prohibition of aid to parochial schools, and of delegates from the Cook County Democratic organization — even from the mayor's office — who voted against proposals with clear organization sponsorship. The delegates cherished their independence and the nonpartisan character of their election, even though such nonpartisan choice was, in some cases, more ostensible than real.

In these and other respects the convention was uniquely of high merit. To one who has observed the Illinois General Assembly for several decades, the qualitative superiority of the constitutional convention over the Illinois legislature was impressive.

The Education Committee shared all these unique advantages. The preplanning studies were most useful, especially the lengthy chapter by Dr. Orville Alexander in *Con-Con: Issues.* The committee also benefited from extensive studies — especially those dealing with the proposed state board of education — by the Illinois State Chamber of Commerce, the Illinois Congress of Parents and Teachers (PTA), the Illinois Education Association, and the principal state school officials. And surely, as Ms. Buresh's comments demonstrate, the members of the Education Committee were themselves of superior quality and dedication.

Thus it is not surprising that the Education Committee produced a superior draft and that its recommendations were accepted by the convention and the voters, with relatively minor change. Ms. Buresh describes these successes and suggests something of their importance. The committee's judgment in its retention of section 3, Public Funds for Sectarian Purposes Forbidden, was a major factor in securing voter approval of the entire document. *Any* change in this section — whether it weakened or strengthened the section — would have aroused serious emotional objection to the document, and might have jeopardized its ratification (just as a clause dealing with school prayer had helped defeat the proposed 1922 Illinois Constitution).

The long and sometimes demoralizing task of defining educational objectives in section 1, Goal — Free Schools, finally resulted in a new emphasis on education. That section states one of the broadest delineations of purpose contained in any state constitution. Professional educators, in Illinois and other states, are delighted with its scope and vision. Even with "*the* paramount" changed first to "*a* paramount" then to "*a fundamental*" goal, the language is impressive. And the final clause in the section, giving the state "the primary responsibility for financing the system of public education," is something like reaching for the stars. Of course, as Ms. Buresh points out, even the sponsors of these rather grandiose goals recognized them to be merely "hortatory." They are still appropriate to a constitution and worded in a way to generate pride.

But the Education Committee's chief task was to provide for a new structure of state management of education through the crea-

tion of a state board of education and the elimination of the popu-
larly-elected, partisan-tinged state superintendent of public instruction. For many citizens concerned with public education this was the
chief task of the convention itself. It was not easy. There was serious
opposition to taking from the voters the choice of the chief state
school officer. While civic groups argued for the short ballot, it is
worth noting that the convention did not find it possible to remove
from the elective process the secretary of state, the attorney general,
the state treasurer, or the comptroller (the former state auditor).
Thus only the Education Committee was able to remove a major
state office from the popular election method.

It is true that, in submitting section 2, State Board of Education
— Chief State Educational Officer, the Education Committee was
unable to agree on two crucial points: the scope of authority and
the manner of selection. Neither was the convention able to resolve
these differences. The result was that both controversies were passed
along for later legislative determination. While there are persons
who will, with some justification, call this a "cop-out," there are
also sound bases for contending that it is wise to leave the legislature
free to decide both issues, retaining full power to alter their choices
if that appears desirable. And this is wholly consistent with the re-
peated wishes of the constitutional "purists," who sought a short,
flexible document. Many delegates were genuinely committed to
this position, and to them section 2 represents work exceedingly well
done.

One must not neglect that real contribution the Education Committee, and the convention, made in deleting sections 2, 4, and 5
of the 1870 article. None of these were properly matters for inclusion in a basic document and each of them had caused some
legal and practical anomalies. But striking them was complex and
difficult.

In its totality, the new education article is vastly superior to the
one it replaced. The story of this enterprise is admirably told in Ms.
Buresh's volume.

RICHARD G. BROWNE
*Staff Counsel, Committee
on Education, Sixth Illinois
Constitutional Convention*

A FUNDAMENTAL GOAL

I

The Education Committee:
Composition and Procedure

All state constitutions set forth the general structure which government is to take, and all provide for a division of that structure into three branches. There is less unanimity among state constitutions as to what specific functions and powers state and local governments are to be given. This is particularly true in the area of education, for although most state constitutions include an education article, opinion is divided on whether such a provision is necessary or even desirable. Since education is one of the areas reserved for state government by the federal Constitution, any reference to it in the constitution limits, rather than extends, the power of the state legislature. If a state constitution remains silent on the subject of education, the only restrictions on the state legislature in handling the area are the general provisions of the federal Constitution or indirect restrictions in the state charter.

When the Sixth Illinois Constitutional Convention was called, Illinois had had three constitutions since its establishment in 1818, only the last of which had included an education article. By November of 1968, when the voters of Illinois approved the calling of the convention, the existing education article shared an obsolescence common to many portions of the 1870 constitution. Criticisms had been leveled at almost all of its articles. The state's revenue and taxing provisions were outdated and inequitable. In some cases, compliance was impossible and the provisions were simply ignored.

Since 1870 eight attempts had been made to amend this article, and all had failed. The judicial article, although completely revised by a 1962 amendment, was the object of attack for its provision for elected judges. The organization and procedures of the General Assembly were archaic and cumbersome. The provisions for reapportionment were ineffective and possibly, in light of the one man–one vote Supreme Court decision, unconstitutional. The relationship between the state and its local governments needed modernization and redefinition to take account of twentieth century urbanization and its attendant problems. And finally, the article providing for constitutional amendment was itself overdue for revision.

Concerning the 1870 education article in particular, there were few criticisms prior to the 1969 convention because most legal and constitutional experts had not given attention to the topic. The ban on aid to nonpublic education was probably the most controversial part of the article, but the debate centered around the legislature, where bills were regularly introduced to allow some form of financial assistance. In the months preceding the convention, only one Chicago newspaper mentioned specifically the need for revision in the constitutional provisions dealing with education. One article suggested the desirability of appointing, rather than continuing to elect, the state superintendent of public instruction, and another asked for a revision of the tax burden so the state would be able to provide more money for schools.[1]

The most insistent demands for change came from educational experts, who had long been seeking various reforms which they now hoped a constitutional convention could accomplish. In particular these experts advocated the creation of a state board of education that would make long-range policies for education in the state and would appoint the state's chief educational officer. In addition, those who felt strongly one way or the other on the issue of state aid to nonpublic schools hoped the constitutional convention would reconsider this problem.

After voter approval of the calling of a convention, the next step was the election of delegates. The 1870 constitution provided that two delegates be elected from each of Illinois's senatorial districts, subject to the same qualifications as state senators. At the time of

[1] *Chicago Sun-Times*, February 25, 1968 and October 3, 1968.

the election Illinois had fifty-eight senatorial districts. Eighteen districts were in the city of Chicago, six in Cook County outside Chicago, and thirty-four outside of Cook County. The legislature, on the recommendation of the Constitution Study Commission and with urging from bar associations, newspapers, and civic groups, decided that the election would be nonpartisan. Although no party designations appeared on the ballot, the major political parties endorsed candidates, as did other political groups — such as the Independent Voters of Illinois, the Illinois Agricultural Association, the Independent Precinct Organization, the Independent Democratic Coalition, the Illinois Communist Party, and the National Socialist Alliance. One newspaper breakdown of the party alignment of the 116 delegates showed fifty-six Republican-endorsed candidates, forty-seven Democratic-endorsed candidates, and thirteen Independent candidates.[2]

The convention met in Springfield; its organization took shape during the first weeks of December 1969. The office of president was created and given broad executive and administrative powers. Samuel W. Witwer, a Republican from Kenilworth and longtime advocate of constitutional reform, was elected president. Three vice-presidents were provided for and elected: Thomas G. Lyons, a Chicago Democrat, Elbert S. Smith, a Republican from Decatur, and John Alexander, a Republican from Virden (at twenty-seven one of the youngest members of the convention). The convention elected Odas Nicholson, a black Democrat from Chicago, to serve as secretary.

The committee structure grew directly out of a set of proposed rules drafted for the convention by a legislative study commission and approved by the convention's Temporary Rules Committee. Nine substantive committees were established: bill of rights, legislative, executive, judiciary, revenue and finance, suffrage and constitutional amendment, local government, general government, and education. Three procedural committees were also created: rules

[2] *Chicago Tribune,* November 19, 1969. Other Chicago newspapers came up with slightly different figures. The *Chicago Daily News* and the *Chicago Sun-Times* reported 58 Republicans, 5 independent Republicans, 39 Democrats, 11 independent Democrats, and 3 Independents (November 20, 1969). *Chicago Today* said the figures were 51 Republicans, 42 Democrats, 21 Independents, and 2 undetermined (November 19, 1969).

and credentials; style, drafting, and submission; and public information.

The inclusion of a committee on education was not without controversy. At the planning sessions of the Constitution Study Commission there had been a movement to eliminate an education committee from the convention and thus an education article from the
constitution. The move was led by Commission member Samuel
K. Gove of the University of Illinois, who felt that an education
committee might make provisions for higher education which would
prove detrimental to education beyond the secondary level. In addition he did not consider education a necessary part of a constitution.
Gove was adamantly opposed by Witwer — also a Commission
member — who felt a committee should be established to deal with
the education article in the 1870 constitution; Witwer was especially concerned with the controversial ban on aid to nonpublic
schools, which was seen as one of the most emotional, and thus one
of the most potentially destructive, issues at the convention. Gove's
proposal was defeated and an education committee was proposed
and established.

The Members

Under his powers as chief executive officer, President Witwer had
full authority after consultation with the vice-presidents to appoint
committee members, chairmen, and vice-chairmen. These appointments were subject to approval by a majority of the members of
the convention. The president himself was a nonvoting member of
each substantive committee, and each vice-president was an ex
officio member of three substantive committees.

There were eleven members on the Education Committee, including the chairman and vice-chairman. Ideological differences
and a complex of other factors soon split the committee into two
factions with differing ideas as to the amount of reform that should
be included in the final education article. This division was recognized not only by members of the committee but also by the press,
which dubbed the two groups the "Young Turks" and the "Old
Guard."[3] The Young Turks were a social group as well as a com-

---

[3] Tony Abel, of WCIA-TV in Champaign, Illinois, was apparently the first
to use the term in press coverage of the committee.

mittee faction with close friendships formed among their members —
a camaraderie which made voting against one another very difficult.

If this group of strong-willed individuals can be said to have had
a leader, it was Malcolm Kamin, a bright, ambitious, and vociferous lawyer from Chicago, thirty years old, a Democrat, and a Jew.
Kamin was a study in contrasts: his self-confidence and somewhat
brash manner at times galled other committee members, but his
quick and enticing wit made it difficult to remain angry at him for
long. He, much to the distress of President Witwer and the official
parliamentarian, was the convention's self-appointed amateur parliamentarian. As resident expert on *Alice in Wonderland* he amused
the convention as often as he irritated it. His unpredictability extended even into the political realm, and his positions on issues were
often a source of speculation among other delegates. Although
seemingly a liberal in conscience, Kamin was a member of the
Chicago Democratic organization and had political ambitions which
caused him to support at times positions he opposed — though not
on educational issues. He seemed able to convince himself that his
final positions were consistent with his philosophy, but others remained skeptical. Most transgressions were forgiven him, however,
due to his exuberant personality, his sense of humor, and his obvious
grasp of complex issues even in fields outside of his experience.

Kamin consulted most frequently on matters of committee strat-
egy with another Young Turk, Franklin Dove of Shelbyville. Dove
was the grandson of a delegate to the ill-fated 1920–22 Illinois
Constitutional Convention and was following the family tradition
of liberal political activity. He was thirty-four years old, a Democrat, and a Protestant. Because his interests lay elsewhere, he was
bitterly disappointed with his appointment to the Education Committee; but once he became enthused about his task he was one of
the committee's most influential members. Dove's quiet demeanor
at the convention, an aspect which was quite misleading to anyone
who did not know him well, hid a shrewd mind which grasped the
core of every issue. It is to him and to Kamin that most of the credit
is due for the careful wording of the new sections of the education
article. Not as flamboyant as Kamin, Dove had an air of gravity
which helped the Young Turks to be taken more seriously by the
older members of the committee and by the convention itself.

If Kamin and Dove were responsible for the exact wording of the new sections of the proposed education article, Samuel Patch was responsible for its spirit. Patch was a colorful, articulate black, a former teacher and city employee from Chicago, age thirty-seven, a Democrat, and a Protestant. He regaled the committee and the convention with his constant exhortation, "You've got to make it real!" — a phrase in vogue at the time on the Springfield scene. Totally pledged to education as a means of providing increased opportunities for black children, Patch, unlike other members of the Young Turks, was optimistic about the chances of writing an excellent education article. He was less cognizant of or less influenced by the limitations of a constitution, and thus less pessimistic about the significance of the outcome of the article. It was his enthusiasm that helped the other younger members eventually to take a greater interest in writing a new article.

The member of the committee closest to Sam Patch was William Fogal, a young political science professor from Pekin, thirty-six years old, a Democrat, and a Protestant. Patch seemed to sense in Fogal a commitment to education as zealous as his own, but Fogal attributed his own enthusiasm almost solely to Patch's influence. Extremely sensitive and shy, Fogal spoke up in committee only when he had something substantive to contribute. His cordial manner endeared him not only to the younger committee members but also to the Old Guard, and it is likely that without his intermediary efforts the rift which developed between the two factions in the committee would never have been healed.

Of the three women on the committee, Betty Howard of St. Charles was certainly the most articulate. She was thirty-nine years old and a Protestant. An advertising and public relations executive, Howard was accustomed to having her opinions heeded by both males and females, and was one of the convention's most ardent sponsors of the women's rights section of the proposed bill of rights. Although a Republican from a largely Republican district, she held views in committee that placed her with the Young Turks, all the rest of whom were Democrats. At the convention itself she seemed more at home with other liberal Republicans than with the Democrats. When the convention moved its location to the Old State

Capitol in March 1970, Howard delighted members by appearing in a costume that might have been worn when the building was dedicated in the mid–nineteenth century. Her presence on the committee, in addition to adding zest, prevented the two sides from being seen as completely Republican versus Democratic factions.

The last delegate who might be considered a member of the Young Turk faction was Gloria Pughsley, an employee of the city of Chicago, and the committee's other black member. She was fifty-four years old, a Protestant, and a Democrat. None of the committee members came to know Pughsley well, as she was ill during most of the committee meetings. When she did speak, she spoke emotionally; her only significant impact at committee meetings was swelling the voting strength of the Young Turk faction. At the full convention she voted strictly with the Chicago Democratic organization.

Chairman Paul Mathias was the leader of the Old Guard faction. Mathias was an able lawyer from Bloomington, age sixty-seven, a Protestant, and a Republican. Like many members of the Young Turks, Mathias was nonplussed by his appointment to the Committee on Education. He might have become an effective informal as well as formal leader had the committee not become divided into factions, and had not his occasionally abrasive manner and his obvious displeasure with most of the proposals of the Young Turks prevented him from gaining power over the younger members. Because Mathias was a member of the Citizens Advisory Committee to the Board of Higher Education and had been legal counsel to the Illinois Board of Regents, he was seen as tied to higher education and his recommendations in this area were met with suspicion by the entire committee. In other areas of education, however, his lead was followed by the Old Guard. Since his interests lay elsewhere, he at times tended to rush consideration of educational matters, and this was a further source of irritation to the Young Turks. Mathias was greatly respected at the convention and was often consulted by President Witwer, especially because of his influence in agricultural circles.

The most winsome member of the committee was J. Lester Buford, at seventy-two the convention's oldest delegate. A former superintendent of schools from Mount Vernon, Buford had long been a highly regarded leader in education in southern Illinois. He was a Protestant and a Republican. Buford was well liked by all members of the committee, but was seen by the Young Turks as a member of the educational establishment.[4] His inexhaustible supply of anecdotes and joviality, however, often helped to ease tension. Like William Fogal of the younger group, Buford became very desirous of healing the wounds which developed within the committee, and his efforts to reach compromise brought him closer to the Young Turks.

Louis Bottino from Wilmington was one of the quieter delegates; in the committee that discussed aid to nonpublic schools, few delegates realized he was a Catholic. His reserve was constant except in discussions on financing the public schools, when he berated the committee for not giving close enough attention to the subject. Bottino, a Republican, age fifty-three, was a college professor and a former legislator and county superintendent of schools. His views were probably more liberal than his voting record would indicate, for he was originally a member of the Young Turk faction but switched sides when controversy began. He often appeared to be caught in a vise between his own conscience and the wishes of his more conservative constituents.

Anne Evans, a housewife from Des Plaines, was the committee's vice-chairman. Age forty-five, a Protestant, and an independent Republican, she became a mother to all of the members. She sincerely worried about them, their health, and their problems. Her sensitive soul was appalled by the breakdown in committee relations but she did not become a successful peacemaker. Although she had been thought to be a liberal Republican, she voted with the Old Guard faction because she had more faith in their opinions on educational matters. Evans was one of the most conscientious of the

[4] During the convention the term "educational establishment" was used to refer to the traditional organized groups concerned with educational policy making, such as the Illinois Parent-Teachers Association, the Illinois Education Association, boards of education, and the Illinois School Problems Commission, as well as individuals who had made their careers in the administration of educational facilities. (Persons whose acquaintance with the Illinois Education Association is recent may be surprised to see it listed with the educational establishment. At the outset of the convention, however, it was still a very conservative operation.)

committee members and could often be found in the committee office doing research on issues with which she was unfamiliar.

Clyde Parker, age sixty-six, a Protestant, and a Republican from Lincolnwood, was perhaps the most inflexible member of the committee. He had a doctoral degree in education, and preferred to be called "Doctor." He had long been associated with education as a professor and as a superintendent of schools. By his own admission, the views he had developed over the years were not changed by anything he heard in committee or at the convention. Because of his long, rambling speeches and his orientation to the educational establishment, the Young Turks came to regard him as an impediment to educational reform and to feel that he did not comprehend the real issues involved. Parker, in turn, was overly suspicious of the younger members and felt that Chicago's Mayor Daley was trying to gain something "sneaky" through the proposals of that group. Due to his background it is not surprising that Parker was conservative on educational matters, and the Young Turks turned resentment they felt toward his conservative stance into resentment for what they termed the whole educational establishment.

While not properly a member of the committee, Dr. Richard G. Browne, the committee counsel, was himself an unsuccessful candidate for delegate and took a great interest in the content of the article. Although his sense of humor and wealth of knowledge endeared him to the members, he was a former executive director of the Illinois Board of Higher Education and this experience in the educational establishment tended to cast him with the Old Guard in the minds of the younger faction. When asked, Browne was not reticent in expressing his opinions, which generally placed him with the Old Guard.

The composition of the Education Committee can be broken down as follows: there were two blacks and nine whites; eight men and three women; five downstate delegates, three suburban Cook County delegates, and three Chicago delegates; three Chicago Democrats, two downstate Democrats, five downstate or suburban Republicans, and one who called herself an Independent but voted with the Republicans; five educators, three lawyers, and two city employees; nine Protestants, a Jew, and a Catholic. All were college graduates, and the median age was forty-nine.

FRUSTRATION AND FACTIONALISM

Appointments to the Committee on Education were the subject of much discussion and not a little dissatisfaction. Education was a committee deemed very important by President Witwer. During meetings of the Constitution Study Commission created by the legislature, he fought for a committee devoted to education, and those who assisted him with committee assignments say he gave it the same attention he gave other committees in regard to political, ethnic, geographical, and sexual representation. The only additional criterion he considered was that the chairman must be one who had no strong views for or against aid to nonpublic schools. The delegates, however, were not privy to this information, and to them the facts seemed to tell a very different story.

The Chicago Democrats were in the minority on the Education Committee as they were on all the committees. Though the composition looked balanced when downstate Democrats were counted, the Chicago Democrats were greatly displeased. They considered their downstate colleagues unknown quantities whose votes could not be counted upon. There were surprisingly few of the convention's thirteen blacks on a committee dealing with an area of such great concern to minority groups, and the single Catholic was also surprising, since Catholics made up over a quarter of the whole delegate body. Although it was asserted by sources close to Witwer that the small Catholic representation was not a deliberate attempt to influence the committee's output, nothing could alter the fact that aid to nonpublic schools was to be in the hands of an overwhelmingly Protestant committee.

While commentators outside the committee may have been concerned over demographic facts such as these, many of the members had a different complaint. Even at the early point when committee appointments were made, it was felt that education — except for the subject of aid to nonpublic schools — would be one of the least controversial, least political, and least divided committees, and thus one on which it would be least important to serve.[5]

The delegates had several reasons for wanting to serve at the convention: the wish to be part of a historic occasion, the hope

[5] Observations about delegate reaction to committee appointments are drawn from the interviews and questionnaire described in the Preface to this volume.

that participation would further a career in politics, the desire to serve a political party or private organization, and the belief that they had some special expertise to contribute to the creation of the new document. Except for the last reason, which education experts could realize, it was believed that none of the ambitions could be satisfactorily fulfilled by being a member of the Committee on Education. Because education was not considered to be a political issue, it would draw little attention and would not further political careers. Even the feeling of participating in a historic occasion would be diminished by serving on a committee of little importance. In selecting committees on which they wished to serve, only five of the 116 delegates made Education their first choice. (By contrast, the Local Government and Revenue Committees were the first choice of twenty-five and twenty-eight delegates, respectively.)

Of the members of the Committee on Education, only five of the eleven claimed to be pleased with their appointments. Delegates Buford and Parker felt they had knowledge to furnish on the subject. Delegates Patch and Pughsley believed education to be an extremely important area for minority groups. The Education Committee was Howard's second preference, and she seems to have been satisfied with her assignment. The remaining members of the committee felt their expertise lay in other fields and were generally upset by the appointments. In completing a questionnaire distributed by the author,[6] they indicated disappointment, frustration, and anger in response to the query: "What was your initial reaction to your assignment to the Education Committee?" These delegates believed their committee to be a catch-all for whoever was left after the other committee appointments had been made. This feeling was reinforced by the fact that two members, Parker and Evans, were from the same district — which seemed to them a result of lack of careful geographic planning in Education Committee assignments. Although their supposition may have been groundless in view of other demographic considerations, these delegates believed themselves neglected and underrated.

There also existed, at the start of the meetings, a sense of futility, especially among the younger members of the Education Commit-

---

[6] See Preface to this volume for a description of this questionnaire, which was completed by all members of the Committee on Education.

tee. With the exception of the section on aid to nonpublic schools, it was thought that there were no substantive issues to discuss. Modernization of the language presented no challenge. Most recommendations at the constitutional level would be merely hortatory words containing no mandate; goals would be stated, but there would be no provisions to require the General Assembly to comply. Feelings of futility appeared to develop not from the belief that education was insignificant but rather from the opinion that little could be done about it on the constitutional level. Thus the committee felt itself, not education, to be inconsequential. The older delegates on the committee were less subject to this feeling of fruitless effort; they would have been content to remove anachronisms and to provide for a state board of education. The younger members wanted to force innovation and to create an article that would "make a difference." At the inception of committee meetings, however, these younger delegates sensed that, given what they perceived to be a conservative delegate body, a committee on which members of the educational establishment were well represented, and general public resistance to constitutional change (typified by the recent defeat of proposed constitutions in three other states), innovation would be difficult to accomplish.

The perceptions of these two groups, the older and the younger, became crucial in creating and maintaining the two factions in the committee. The Old Guard opted for modernization of the language of Article VIII, the provision of some slight degree of flexibility for the future, the removal of anachronisms, and the creation of structures that had long been the goals of educational experts. The Young Turks, less imbued with educational experience but unwilling to rely on the expertise of the older delegates, chose to work for innovation in addition to the modernization asked for by the Old Guard. They seemed to be saying with Rousseau: "People are always telling me to make PRACTICAL suggestions. You might as well tell me to suggest what people are doing already, or at least to suggest improvements which may be incorporated with the wrong methods at present in use."[7] The futility felt by the Young Turks led them to seek more radical solutions to educational diffi-

[7] Jean Jacques Rousseau, *Emile,* trans. Barbara Foxley (London: J. M. Dant & Sons Ltd., 1957), p. 2.

culties. They tended to see the steadfastness of the Old Guard, who were all Republicans, as an outgrowth of partisan hostility.[8] The Old Guard, on the other hand, attempted to seek solutions within the existing system; they were being practical, and they felt their suggestions more closely reflected prevailing public opinion. They were hesitant to open themselves to "radical" new ideas and were more cognizant of the need not to arouse undue opposition from the voters. The Young Turks in their enthusiasm for creating an innovative article were ready to take chances that certain "radical" ideas could be sold to the voters without bringing the document to defeat. Thus, even at the very beginning of committee meetings, the elements were present which would create the conflict over the degree of reform to be included in the new article. Only on the issue of aid to nonpublic schools would most members of both factions agree on what had to be done.

THE DECISION PROCESS

The rules of the convention established the process by which the 1870 Illinois Constitution was to be revised, altered, or amended. Each delegate could draft and submit his suggestions to the convention; these were called member proposals. Five hundred eighty-two member proposals were introduced and read before the assembled delegates and assigned by the President to the appropriate committee. Committees considered member proposals along with research materials prepared in advance of the convention by the Constitution Study Commission and the Governor's Constitution Research Group and during the convention by staff researchers employed by the convention for each committee.

[8] While it is true that most of the Young Turks were Democrats and all of the Old Guard were Republicans, there were other differences which played at least as great, if not a greater, role in the schism between the two groups. The average age of the Young Turks was 38 years, while that of the Old Guard (including Committee Counsel Browne, a Democrat) was 62 years. Furthermore, the Young Turks may have subconsciously resented the much greater educational experience of the older group and the smugness it may have engendered. Meanwhile the Old Guard was apparently incensed at the frequent failure of several of the Young Turks to arrive on time for committee meetings. This was certainly the reaction of Chairman Mathias, who was more than once heard to mutter that the younger members might be on time if they didn't stay up to the early hours of the morning.

Committees also devoted a great deal of time to hearing testimony from expert witnesses, citizens, and interest groups. This was part of a public relations effort which also included "road shows" (local public hearings) held throughout the state. It was widely believed at the convention that the voters should be made to feel involved in the constitution making to develop at the outset favorable public opinion of the convention and the proposed document.

Other steps were taken to insure the involvement of the people. All meetings of the convention were open to the public, and an agenda for each committee meeting had to be posted forty-eight hours in advance. Journals and transcripts were available for public inspection, and delegates were expected to be readily accessible to their constituents. By means of this openness the public was kept informed, their interest was stimulated, and they were made to feel they had a part in the constitution making. In return, the delegates could sense public reaction to various proposals before they made final decisions on what to include in the constitution.

Openness also had disadvantages. Narrow proposals which would benefit only certain interest groups had to be considered. A great deal of redundant and irrelevant testimony was heard. Much attention had to be given to doing things for effect, and the impact of convention decisions on the voters had to be considered. Although openness was time consuming, the delegates would have been unwise to have proceeded differently. They were aware that many proposed constitutions had recently failed to be approved by the voters and they blamed this partly on a lack of public awareness and interest. Public exposure, response, and feedback were integral to their purpose.

After considering ideas from all sources, each committee drew up language for a new article in the constitution. The proposed language, called the committee proposal, was submitted to the convention together with the committee report (the rationale for the proposal). If there were three or more member dissents from the majority proposal, a minority proposal and report — and sometimes many of them — could also be submitted.

The majority and minority proposals of the committees were submitted at first reading, and the proposal which emerged from that stage was subject to two more readings at the full convention.

The convention sat in plenary session for second and third readings; debate was limited and the previous question could be invoked, though the debate-limiting devices were rarely used. After each reading the proposals as amended and approved were sent to the Committee on Style, Drafting, and Submission, where stylistic changes were made. At the end of third reading the delegates gave final approval to the substance and form of the constitution as it was to be submitted for referendum approval by the voters.

The issues to be discussed by the Committee on Education were chosen rather informally by the committee members themselves, and subcommittees were organized around the topics. Forty-four meetings of the Committee on Education were held in Springfield, sometimes jointly with the Bill of Rights or Executive Committees. Early meetings were devoted to the hearing of expert witnesses and to member proposals, and later meetings to debate on the issues and the writing of the final report.

The committee attempted to hear testimony from all educational experts in Illinois as well as from all interested citizens. Although the speakers were important in giving a general sense of group and public feeling, especially on the topic of aid to nonpublic schools, the committee members were influenced very little by witnesses. In fact, questionnaire and interview data indicate that the formal convention machinery to air issues had little effect on the members' views on educational matters. Member proposals were not seen as influential in committee decisions. Determinations on the issues had been made by the members before testimony was even heard on some of the proposals.[9] Subcommittees were created, but they were not perceived by the members as an important part of the committee process. Nor was research: data gathered for the committee in most cases supported decisions already made, and was not seen by the delegates as an important factor for the final committee proposal. In addition, each member stated that he or she had been elected to make his or her own decisions and that wishes of constituents were not the primary factor in positions taken.

It is conceivable that the delegates were swayed by the pressure of interest groups such as the Illinois Education Association, the

---

[9] The committee minutes show votes were taken before testimony was heard on many subjects.

Illinois Congress of Parents and Teachers, or the Illinois Catholic Conference. There was, however, surprisingly little significant pressure from these groups or from most other groups. The issue of financing public schools provoked the only incidents of lobbying in the committee. Representatives of the Illinois State Chamber of Commerce attempted to get delegates to vote against total state financing, while representatives of the Welfare Council of Metropolitan Chicago attempted to gain votes for that same concept. Most educational organizations seemed content to present their positions and then to let the committee handle the situation from there. The only lobby which, while applying no obvious pressure, might be seen as a significant factor in delegate positions is that of higher education; pressures from that source are discussed in some detail in Chapter IV of this volume.

If wishes of constituents were not the primary motivating factors in delegate decisions — if little attention was paid to expert testimony, witnesses, lobbyists, research, member proposals, or subcommittees — then one must look elsewhere for the basis on which decisions were made. The desire not to alarm the voters seems to have been important mainly in controversial areas such as section 3 (aid to nonpublic schools). Most of the older committee members had their minds made up as to educational matters prior to any committee meetings. In response to the question, Do these positions as stated represent your feelings during the whole proceedings or did your positions change? Parker and Buford specifically stated that their many years of experience in the field of education had given rise to the views they held, which were not altered during the convention. All of the members of the Old Guard except Evans, who was less experienced in educational matters, indicated similar positions.

It was only natural that men and women who felt they were experts in the field of education would be hesitant to change viewpoints they had developed over the years, but even the "non-experts" maintained a somewhat inflexible stance. Unlike most members of the Old Guard, the majority of the Young Turks had taken no strong positions on educational matters during their campaigns. Very early in committee meetings, however, the Young Turks developed stands on the issues and were not swayed to any greater degree by research, witnesses, constituents, lobbyists, or member proposals than were the Old Guard. Apparently the Young Turks formed their opinions during early discussions among all members of the committee. In explaining their rigidity, Kamin emphasized that initial discussions among all members of the committee logically led to the section on goals urged by the Young Turks. The Old Guard, although having given lip service to a strong statement of objectives, refused, according to Kamin, to accept proposals based on the viewpoint that the younger members felt had been accepted by all — a viewpoint which recognized the great need for emphasizing the priority of education. Like the Old Guard, the younger members remained convinced of their correctness and logic and refused, for a time, to change or to compromise.

The Young Turks at first attempted to use delaying tactics to postpone final votes until the return of Pughsley, who they were convinced would vote with them. Even if Pughsley failed to come back to break the stalemate, the Young Turks knew they might win if they delayed final votes long enough to force the Old Guard to accept their wording. The younger members felt the solidarity of their group was greater than that of the Old Guard. They expected that some of the older delegates would eventually give in, thus breaking the five-to-five stalemate and allowing majority and minority reports to be written. If the Old Guard did not split apart, there was still the prospect of Pughsley's arrival to give the victory to the younger members. Feeling that the ultimate triumph would be theirs, the Young Turks savored being on a team and scheming against an adversary.

The factions in the Committee on Education were formed by differing viewpoints and conflicting feelings about the significance and potential of the committee. Once they had coalesced, those factions took on an exaggerated importance in the minds of the members. Belonging to a team and defeating the other team became goals in themselves. A game was created, and winning against the opponent became the purpose of playing. Eventually most of the members realized they were playing games and they then subordinated the importance of the factions and games to the larger goal of compromise to draft an education article.

The article the committee finally submitted was drafted so as not to arouse the opposition of the voters; but without the opposition and interaction between the committee's factions, the article's innovative features might never have been achieved. The committee handled five general topics: the structure of the educational system; the objectives of education; higher education; aid to nonpublic schools; and the financing of the public school system. How the eventual compromise between innovation and acceptability was accomplished will become clear in the upcoming chapters, where these five major topics are discussed.

Deleting Portions of the 1870 Article

While very few convention decisions were made without careful thought and debate, the overwhelming majority of delegates shared from the outset the goal of deleting certain material which, in the light of experience, had proved inappropriate for constitutional stature. There were three such sections in Article VIII, the education article, of the 1870 constitution: 2, 4, and 5. Of them, only section 2 proved at all difficult to handle, either in committee or on the floor. That section read:

> All lands, moneys, or other property, donated, granted or received for school, college, seminary or university purposes, and the proceeds thereof, shall be faithfully applied to the objects for which such gifts or grants were made.

As courts had interpreted section 2, its major effect was to prohibit taxation or special assessment of public school property acquired by gift, but only that property acquired prior to 1870. Therefore, the section referred primarily to land acquired in the original grant of land for statehood: section 16 of every township or property acquired by using proceeds from section 16 lands. If school authorities were unable to prove that the land was so acquired, it was subject to taxation.

Committee research showed that most Illinois townships had sold their section 16 lands years ago. A small number, however, kept the proceeds from these sales in a "loanable fund" to be used for school operating expenses. According to Dr. Browne, only seven townships held either in land or in loanable funds as much as $50,000 of these receipts at the time of the convention. The Chicago Board of Education held the largest amount of property under this section, over four-fifths of the total, but the income from such property was only a very small portion of the district budget. The result of the deletion of the provision, the committee found, would be to place school property acquired prior to 1870 in the same category as all other school property used for school purposes, which was exempt from taxation under Article IX, section 3, of the 1870 constitution. Therefore, if such property was being used for school purposes it would not be taxed. If not used for such purposes, it was subject to a "use tax" in any case. Two member proposals were introduced on this subject. Proposal 158 recommended the deletion of section 2, whereas Proposal 498 suggested a slight rewording of the section.

The April 8 vote in committee to eliminate the provision was unanimous. The proposed deletion, however, caused sufficient controversy when the first committee proposal reached the floor of the convention for first reading on April 28, to cause Mathias to ask for time for further consideration by the committee. On April 30 Delegate Thomas McCracken, an employee in the office of Cook County Assessor P. J. Cullerton, spoke to the committee and advised deletion. Since most of the disagreement had come from persons in the Chicago area, and since McCracken had presumably consulted with his employer and with the Chicago Board of Education, his suggestion was followed; when section 2 was again brought before the whole convention on May 6, the committee's recommendation was to delete. As explained in the committee report:

> The subject lies basically in the realm of inter-governmental taxation and is properly an issue for legislation. . . .
> The total impact of the section is so slight that the Committee does not consider it to warrant a place in the Constitution.

Section 4, prohibiting any school officer from being interested in the sale of "any book, apparatus or furniture" used in the schools, was easily disposed of. On March 24 the first vote on the section was taken; the decision to delete it was unanimous. As stated in the committee report:

> The Committee on Education does not suggest that carefully drafted conflict of interest prohibitions may not be appropriate

in educational institutions as elsewhere. But the Committee is convinced that such provisions are properly legislative in character and should not appear in the Constitution. The Committee heard no evidence to the contrary.

Similarly, section 5, which provided that there may be superintendents of schools in each county, was omitted. There had recently been serious question raised as to the necessity for such an office. At the time of the 1970 convention there were five counties with only one school district, eight with two school districts, and in forty-five other counties the number of districts was less than ten. Only thirteen of the 102 counties had more than twenty school districts.

Since the constitution did not require county superintendents of schools, comprehensive legislation was passed in 1969 recognizing the greatly changed nature of this office in these days of reorganized and consolidated school districts. The bill changed the title of the office to Superintendent of Educational Service Region, and authorized the combining of two or more counties beginning in August of 1971. By August of 1973 all counties of fewer than sixteen thousand population were to have merged with neighboring counties to form a region. By 1977 all counties of fewer than thirty-three thousand must combine. Thus, the number of educational service regions was to be substantially reduced, as had been advocated for years by educational experts.

On March 24 a final vote was taken on section 5: eight favored deletion, one (Bottino) opposed deletion, and one (Buford) voted present. The motion to strike having received a majority, the section was removed with the understanding that the committee would recommend creation of an intermediate office by law. Bottino gave no explanation in committee or in answer to a questionnaire for his vote. He had previously been a county superintendent of schools, however, which may explain his desire to see that office continue to receive constitutional recognition. Buford remarked at the meeting on March 24 that he agreed with Bottino, but gave no reason then or later for his opinion.

II

Creating a State Board of Education

That the convention would create a state board of education was the hope of almost all educational experts and organizations. At the time of the 1970 convention, Illinois and Wisconsin were the only states without a state board to research and institute long-range school policies.

In Illinois for many years the School Problems Commission, made up of five senators and five representatives appointed by the leadership of those bodies, and five laymen appointed by the governor, with the superintendent of public instruction and the director of finance serving as ex officio members, had attempted to operate in this capacity; however, its policy-making function was limited to making recommendations to the General Assembly. The Commission had been created in 1947 and continued by a series of acts until 1957 when it became permanent. It was the School Problems Commission which, in 1963, recommended the creation of a state board of education; the 1966 Illinois Task Force on Education, a group appointed jointly by Governor Kerner, Superintendent of Public Instruction Ray Page, and the Commission made the same recommendation. All efforts at creating such a board by statute or by constitutional provision had failed, and in 1969 the report of the School Problems Commission read: "This perennial question has been raised frequently during the many hearings. [It] is nearly always related to the selection of the Superintendent of Public Instruction. The Commission feels that this question should be faced and solved by the Constitutional Convention."[1]

Several reasons had been given over time for the creation of a state board of education. The General Assembly, it was said, does not have sufficient time to study adequately all the proposals which come before it, and a state board of education could provide valuable assistance by studying school problems, proposing solutions, and analyzing the effect of school legislation. The state board of education could coordinate the work of various committees and commissions which deal with specific educational problems. With long-term, overlapping membership, such a board could provide continuity in long-range planning and study and could evaluate the results of its recommendations and policies, thus eliminating the need for much emergency and temporary legislation. In addition, recommendations of such a board would supposedly be given more attention by the General Assembly than those of a single elected official or of regional or interest groups, because a properly composed state board would be representative of all people in the state. It was also agreed that the General Assembly is more likely to give adequate power to such a board than to an official chosen on a partisan ballot. Finally, a state board would provide the public with a visible and continuing body to which it could bring its school problems.

Many of these arguments could have been used to support the continuance of the School Problems Commission, which proposed legislation and studied educational matters. It was conceivable that a state board of education would have no more extensive powers than the Commission. However, advocates of the creation of the board pointed out that the majority of members on the Commission were elected officials with other responsibilities and loyalties, that the Commission had an inadequate staff, and that its existence was at the discretion of the legislature. In addition, the Commission itself had never assumed that it should be concerned with educational problems except those that could be dealt with by appropriate legislation.[2] Presumably, the scope and interest of a state

---

[1] Illinois, School Problems Commission, *Report* (Springfield, 1969), p. 5.
[2] Orville Alexander, "Education," in *Con-Con: Issues for the Illinois Constitutional Convention,* ed. Samuel K. Gove and Victoria Ranney (Urbana: University of Illinois Press, 1970), p. 441.

board would be broader since its members would have no other responsibilities and since policy making and evaluation would be part of its job.

ELECTION OR APPOINTMENT?

As noted in the School Problems Commission report, controversy over the manner of selection of the superintendent of public instruction was one of the main obstacles to the creation of a state board. In 1854 the office of superintendent of education was created by statute; the superintendent was to be appointed by the governor for a two-year term. The constitution of 1870 changed the name of the office to superintendent of public instruction and made it an elective, four-year position. Numerous experts had since suggested that an officer with such heavy responsibility for the schools should not be subjected to the necessity of running in a partisan election every four years. The elective aspect of the office had been under attack since as early as 1915, when the report of the Efficiency and Economy Committee pointed out that popular election was not the proper way to select a professional to head the state's educational system. Critics had also noted that the elective nature of the position led to political patronage, especially since the office was one of the few specifically exempt from the state's personnel code, which governs the amount of patronage permitted.

Another obstacle to the creation of a state board of education was the controversy over the manner in which board members would be selected. The 1963 recommendation of the School Problems Commission was that board members be appointed by the governor. The 1966 Task Force on Education also suggested the appointment of members but later amended its report to favor not stipulating a method of selection, preferring to leave the matter to the legislature.[3]

Research done for the Committee on Education by Dr. Browne gleaned the following information concerning selection of the board members. Thirty-two states had boards appointed by the governor. Of these, sixteen were selected with the consent of the senate, twelve were appointed by the governor alone, three were appointed with the consent of an advisory council, and one was appointed with the

[3] Illinois, Task Force on Education, *Education for the Future of Illinois* (Springfield, 1966), p. 60.

consent of the legislature. In eleven states the members of the board were selected by popular election. In Hawaii, Nebraska, Nevada, Ohio, and Utah the election was on a nonpartisan basis, whereas partisan designations appeared on the ballots of Colorado, Kansas, Louisiana, Michigan, New Mexico, and Texas. A few states had other methods of selecting board members. In New York and South Carolina members were elected by the legislature; in Florida and Mississippi the board was made up of elected officials ex officio; and in Washington the board was chosen by the board of directors of local school districts.

Not all forty-eight states that had boards provided for their manner of selection in their constitutions. The composition of the boards was determined by statute in twenty-nine states. Of the states which stipulated the manner of selection in their constitution, nine provided for election and eight for appointment. The two states with ex officio boards provided for this constitutionally.

Popular election of the chief state school officer was at one time the method of selection used in most of the states. By 1970, however, only twenty states continued to use this system. Between 1945 and 1970, numerous states had changed from electing this officer to appointing him, but no state had switched from appointment to election.

Six member proposals presented to the convention (8, 53, 90, 161, 267, 367) dealt with the establishment of a state board of education. All asked that such a board be created, and all but one recommended that the board appoint the superintendent of public instruction. The one exception, Member Proposal 367, did not mention such an official. If the proposals were any indication of delegate feeling, it appeared there would be little controversy about the creation of a state board which would appoint the chief educational officer. This sense of unanimity was reinforced by the testimony of witnesses: of forty-three who spoke on the subject, forty-one favored creation of such a board.

Although in agreement as to the need for such a board, the member proposals differed as to the manner of selection of its members. Three of the proposals asked that the board be elected, two of these (8 and 267) recommending election of one member from each congressional district, while the third (53) suggested the creation of fifteen special districts for such election. Two other proposals (90 and 161) left the manner of selection of the board to the legislature, while the sixth proposal (367) asked that the board be appointed by the governor.

The argument over election versus appointment of the superintendent and other state officials appeared time and again during the course of the convention. Those who favored appointment of the state superintendent felt that few qualified individuals have the political expertise to run for election, or wish to risk their careers or spend the money needed for a political campaign; those who do become candidates are usually supported by a political party and are answerable to that party after the election. It was also noted that, with a proliferation of elective offices, voters do not have the time or the information to make the best selection among candidates. The same concerns were expressed in consideration of method of selection of other officials throughout the convention. In addition, those favoring appointment felt the state's chief educational officer, especially, should be chosen for his professional qualifications rather than for his vote-getting ability and while in office should be concerned with the job before him rather than with reelection.

The argument in favor of elective rather than appointive offices was generally that of leaving the power to the people.[4] It was also thought that officers who were chosen in popular elections would be more responsive to the popular will. Proponents of appointment cited studies of accountability in state government that brought into question the premise that effective control by the people is achieved through a long ballot of elected officials. Nevertheless, the Illinois Federation of Teachers, the only significant organization in Illinois which opposed creation of a state board of education, apparently based its resistance on the appointment of the state's chief educational officer, which it saw as concomitant with the creation of the board. Delegate Dwight Friedrich, a member of the Execu-

[4] According to a 1918 history of Illinois constitutional conventions, increasing the number of popularly elected officers was intended to give the people greater control over the administration of the state government. Illinois Legislative Reference Bureau, *Constitutional Conventions in Illinois* (Springfield: Schnepp and Barnes, 1919), p. 44.

tive Committee, was a leader in seeking to keep the office elective, and it was consideration of this issue which led to a joint meeting of the Education and Executive Committees.

The general agreement among organizations and witnesses in favor of the creation of a state board of education broke down over the manner of selection of the board members. Of the forty-one witnesses who spoke in favor of a state board of education, four were in favor of an elected board, fourteen were in support of an appointed board (most mentioned appointment by the governor), and twenty-three felt that the manner of selection should be left to the General Assembly. Some of the witnesses were speaking as individual laymen, but most were educational experts or representatives of organizations with an interest in education.

The arguments given for an elected state board of education were similar to those mentioned above in regard to the election of a chief state educational officer; those favoring an appointed board gave reasons similar to the reasons for the appointment of such an officer. An example of the arguments for an appointed board was provided by the Illinois Congress of Parents and Teachers:

> Our preference is for a Board which is appointed by the Governor with the assistance of a selection committee. We do not believe there is any way for members of a State Board of Education to be elected which can entirely by-pass the political machinery in both the nominating and electing process.

Witnesses seemed to feel that education, unlike the other aspects of state government, must be kept out of partisan politics. This was a frequently recurring theme throughout discussions of all aspects of the article.

Most of the research materials and witnesses appeared to favor leaving the manner of selection of the state board to the legislature but giving the board the power to appoint the state's chief educational officer. The witnesses based their arguments for legislative selection of the board on one or both of the following: first, that neither election nor appointment could be shown to be superior to the other, and second, that neither method should be frozen into the constitution, preventing change at a later date.

In committee testimony not one reform or good government

group (such as the League of Women Voters or the Urban League) was in favor of an elected state board. This was a trend noticeable throughout the convention: reform groups almost always supported appointive methods and the short ballot, whereas the elective system was favored by blacks, party Democrats, and delegates from southern Illinois and small towns, who feared a lack of representation for their regions. Reformers hesitate to insist upon the "democratic" electoral process, for they claim to have found that with the ballot comes partisanship and patronage.[5] This hesitancy is, of course, most evident in discussions of the ostensibly nonpolitical subject of education. As the committee began to consider the issues, it was agreed as to the need for a state board of education, but split on the manner of selection of its members.

JURISDICTION OF THE BOARD

Also undecided at the outset of committee deliberations was the question of the board's jurisdiction. A preliminary vote taken on February 18 showed six members favoring one board for all public education, kindergarten through the university, while four opted for a state board to cover only up to grade twelve. At this point no one was in favor of leaving the matter of the board's jurisdiction to the discretion of the legislature. In regard to the manner of selection of the board, four wanted an elected board, five favored leaving the manner of selection to the General Assembly, and no one desired an appointed board.

The issue of the jurisdiction of the board was not widely discussed prior to the convention. At the time of the convention Illinois had no body governing elementary and secondary education, but many boards dealing with higher education. Committee research indicated that thirty-two of the forty-eight states with state boards of education gave their boards responsibility only through the secondary level; eleven state boards were given additional responsibility for a portion of higher education, and five of the state boards had jurisdiction over all of public education through the university level. Most witnesses did not speak directly to the issue of jurisdiction,

---

[5] This sentiment was expressed by Albert Raby, Wayne Whalen, Peter Tomei, and Anne Evans in interviews with the author, April 1970.

but since the committee was divided on the subject, it was a question often asked of witnesses by committee members. Most responded that they were in favor of two boards, one for education through grade twelve and one for higher education. Among those individuals and organizations taking this position were various representatives of higher education, the Illinois Education Association, the Illinois State Chamber of Commerce, and the Conference on a State Board of Education and an Appointive Superintendent — a group made up of educators and laymen. The reason most frequently given for this stand was that higher and lower education have different problems and different responsibilities.

Professor Gove testified in support of leaving the jurisdiction of the board to the General Assembly, while two other witnesses, Cook County Superintendent of Schools Robert Hanrahan and Superintendent of Public Instruction Ray Page, were in favor of an overall board. On this Page declared:

> After careful evaluation and study I believe that the present proliferation of all phases of education and related areas into a wide variety of boards, commissions, and committees has encouraged and aided duplication and fragmentation of our educational system in the state of Illinois. There is no existing state board dealing with elementary and secondary schools; but to add one more state board for the purpose of dealing with this level of education seems to me to be an extension of the fragmentation which I have referred to.

Two member proposals dealing with the state board mentioned its jurisdiction. Proposal 267 stated:

> The operation and administration of the public school system, including State higher education institutions, shall be the responsibility of a State School Board.

Member Proposal 53 read:

> The State Board of Education has jurisdiction over all public education, through the 14th grade which includes junior colleges.

Proposal 367 was unclear but resembled Proposal 53 in referring to "all institutions established or authorized to provide education and training pursuant to this Article." Delegate Mathias, who wrote Proposal 161, was strongly opposed to a superboard; his wording refers only to "the system of free schools." Proposal 90, written by Fogal, mentioned that the board should have "jurisdiction over all public schools in Illinois." This terminology is vague and could be read to cover education through the university level, as Fogal's voting record in the committee would indicate he intended.

Between the preliminary vote on February 18 and the second vote, on March 4, there was a slight decline in support for a superboard. Only five members (Buford, Dove, Fogal, Howard, and Patch) favored a superboard and four members (Bottino, Evans, Mathias, and Parker) still opposed it; Kamin voted present and Pughsley was absent. The same day, Bottino, Evans, Mathias, and Kamin were willing to let the jurisdiction be provided by law, while the remaining six wanted that decision to be made by the convention. On March 11 a report supporting the committee proposal and written by Dr. Browne was tentatively approved except for the topic of jurisdiction. A hand vote on this date revealed, however, that the number of committee members favoring an overall board had dropped to four. On the next day, Dove submitted tentative wording to which the committee unanimously agreed:

> The board shall establish goals, determine policies, provide for planning and evaluating educational programs, recommend financing and have such jurisdiction, powers and duties as provided by law.

This was not to be the final wording of the committee's proposal, but the delegates had at least agreed that the jurisdiction of the board would be left to the General Assembly — a rather rapid turnabout from the vote of the day before. On February 18 no one had favored leaving the jurisdiction to the legislature; on March 4 six members had opposed this alternative; and on March 11 four still were in opposition. By March 12, however, support was unanimous.

It is possible the sudden change of position was due to a realization that unanimity would not be reached by the committee or by the full convention, and that it would be better to let the legislature decide the issue. Perhaps the delegates realized flexibility was needed in this area. The timing of the changes in position, however, presents another more likely alternative. From February 25 on, sporadic discussion of educational objectives had been taking place in the committee; on March 11, the day before the compromise vote on jurisdiction, the subcommittee on objectives presented its report. Quite possibly, committee members were beginning to realize how difficult it would be to reach agreement on educational objectives and to understand that other problems, such as jurisdiction, would have to be resolved quickly to clear the agenda for that battle.

Kamin's behavior may also have been significant in bringing about a compromise on jurisdiction. The most influential and certainly the most vociferous member of the Young Turks, he had already voted for allowing the jurisdiction to be provided by law. It is quite possible the younger members, now fused into a strong and cohesive group, were influenced by his fear that the representatives of higher education might work for the defeat of the whole article if it contained provisions for a superboard.[6]

A COMPROMISE ON MANNER OF SELECTION

The second structural issue on which there was dissension was that of the manner of selection of the board members. The preliminary vote on February 18 showed four (Howard, Buford, Parker, and Patch) in favor of an elected board and five choosing to leave the manner of selection to the General Assembly. No one at this time voted for an appointed board, although in the author's questionnaire Bottino, Mathias, and Evans favored an appointed board established by the legislature. The vote on March 4 revealed that Howard no longer wished to require an elected board in the constitution, but that Buford, Parker, and Patch still wished to do so. Dove came out in favor of an appointed board stipulated in the constitution, and the remaining delegates voted to leave the issue to the legislature.

On March 11 the subcommittee on structure presented its report on the manner of selection. The subcommittee was divided and was able to report only this division. But, as with jurisdiction, the committee reached an almost unanimous decision the following day on the proposal presented by Dove:

There shall be a state board of education selected on a regional

6 Malcolm Kamin, in an interview with the author, March 12, 1970.

basis. The number of members, their qualifications, terms of office and manner of selection shall be provided by law.

The term "selected," Dove made clear, was intended to mean either elected or appointed.

Parker still voted in favor of an elected board. Patch was not particularly happy, but seemed to prefer voting with the other Young Turks to siding with Parker. Buford was placated by inclusion of the phrase, "on a regional basis," for his greatest fear had been a lack of representation for southern Illinois. Again, this consensus was possible for many reasons. The most likely was that because of the division on the subject of educational goals, there was hesitancy to continue argument on other issues. Most of the committee's time would have to be devoted to attaining agreement on the objectives of education.

By April 8 the divisiveness in the committee generally had been resolved, as will be shown, and unanimous acceptance was given this final wording regarding the state board:

There shall be a State Board of Education selected on a regional basis. The number of members, their qualifications, terms of office and manner of selection shall be provided by law. The Board shall establish goals, determine policies, provide for planning and evaluating educational programs, recommend financing and have such jurisdiction, powers and duties as provided by law.

There shall be a chief state educational officer appointed by the State Board of Education.

III

Formulating Educational Objectives

Article VIII, section 1, of the 1870 constitution read:

> The General Assembly shall provide a thorough and efficient system of free schools, whereby all children of this State may receive a good common school education.

When written in 1870 this was a new constitutional provision for Illinois, for neither the 1818 nor the 1848 constitutions required a statewide school system. Although there had been attempts throughout the years to establish school systems in Illinois by statute, the first really effective school code was not passed until 1845.

Section 1 stipulated the goals for education in 1870. Today this statement seems rather vague, but an examination of the 1870 debates throws some light on the intention of the writers. There were five resolutions presented to the 1870 convention on this subject.[1] The Committee on Education apparently incorporated ideas from all of these resolutions into its section 1, which read:

> The General Assembly shall provide a thorough and efficient system of free schools, whereby all minor children of this State may receive a good common school education.

From remarks made during the debates there seems to have been little controversy in the committee regarding section 1. The schools

---

[1] References to occurrences and conversations at the 1870 Illinois Constitutional Convention are based on *Debates and Proceedings of the Constitutional Convention of the State of Illinois, 1868–1870* (Springfield: E. L. Merritt and Brother, 1870).

were to be thorough, efficient, free, and open to all. This section did cause controversy at the full convention, however. A unanimous motion by the members of the committee to strike the word "minor" as unnecessary met with opposition. Various delegates insisted this word was important to insure that people over twenty-one years of age would not receive education at state expense, but the motion to strike the word passed by a vote of twenty to eighteen. Nevertheless, it was clear from the discussion that most delegates intended only children to be educated under this provision. One delegate said:

> There are three different kinds of education, for only one of which the state provides. ... It is not contemplated that an academic education shall be taught in the common schools, or a collegiate education. ... The academic courses are calculated to prepare one for some particular pursuit in life and so with the collegiate course. Only the common school we propose to make free by general taxation.

The separation of education into the three divisions of common school, academic, and collegiate makes it clear that common school education was to be education of only a rudimentary sort. When someone remarked that the term was very vague, a delegate explained, "The standard of 'common school education' is liable to undergo great changes, and its degree and limited character should not be placed in a constitution." The term was defended, nevertheless, on the grounds that the people of the state understood it and would know that they were not being taxed to provide for institutions of higher learning. Therefore, by their wording in section 1, the delegates to the 1870 convention intended that schools be maintained which were free and open to all persons under twenty-one years of age, that only the rudiments of learning be taught, and that the schools be thorough and efficient.

Although the term "common school education" was outdated in 1969, the question as to what constitutes its meaning had not caused any difficulty, for the courts had been content to interpret it by means of whatever curriculum requirements the legislature established. Yet it is important to note that in 1879, in the case of *Richards* v. *Raymond* (92 Ill. 612, 1879), the courts construed the term to apply also to a high school education, something the 1870 delegates had specifically opposed. To them high school was "academic" education and beyond the basics provided by the common schools.

The question of whether Illinois's school system is "thorough and efficient" had been open to continuing controversy. There had been a gradual trend in Illinois to consolidate and simplify school district organization. These consolidations, brought about by local referendum, were frequently challenged in court on the grounds that such changes would render the schools less "thorough and efficient." The courts usually refused to rule on such challenges, stating that the "thorough and efficient" stipulation was a matter for legislative, not judicial, determination.[2]

There had been little discussion of the wording "all children of the state," which had been read to mean that the school systems must operate uniformly throughout the state and that any particular school district cannot discriminate among its students. The requirement that the schools be free had not caused difficulty except on the subject of free textbooks. According to the interpretation in *Segar* v. *Board of Education* (317 Ill. 418, 1925) schools were not required to supply free textbooks; that ruling was to be the basis for some controversy in the 1970 Committee on Education.

Provisions similar to section 1 of Article VIII are found in the constitutions of thirty-one other states, many in much greater detail. The Model State Constitution, although implying that an education article is not necessary, provides a broad statement of goals:

> The legislature shall provide for the maintenance and support of a system of free public schools open to all children in the state and shall establish, organize and support such other public institutions, including public institutions of higher learning, as may be desirable.[3]

Because the 1870 Illinois section really mandated nothing and granted no new powers to the General Assembly, it was considered

[2] George C. Braden and Rubin G. Cohn, *The Illinois Constitution: An Annotated and Comparative Analysis* (Urbana: Institute of Government and Public Affairs, University of Illinois, 1969), p. 401. See also *People* v. *Deatherage*, 401 Ill. 26 (1948).

[3] National Municipal League, *Model State Constitution* (New York: National Municipal League, 1941), p. 21.

merely hortatory language by most constitutional and educational experts. On the other hand, since one of the main functions of a constitution is to outline general policy, the section could have been regarded as providing the educational goals toward which the state should strive.

A NEW EMPHASIS ON EDUCATION

It was the general feeling among educational experts, witnesses, and committee members during the 1970 convention that section 1 of the 1870 education article was inadequate to express the importance of education in today's world. Faith in education as the eradicator of all evils is often found among both educators and laymen. This seems to be especially true of those who deal with the poor and underprivileged. A statement representative of this faith in education was presented by the Educational Development Cooperative:

> Although we obviously approach these topics with an "educational" bias, our conviction is that true quality education in Illinois can help in solving other pressing state needs: unemployment, welfare, public health, air-water pollution, mental health, minority group problems, and in many aspects of long range planning.

Although this same faith in education had been exhibited by Horace Mann in the 1830s and 1840s and by other educators and laymen in the nineteenth century, the convention of 1870 had apparently given low priority to education and had seen its function as merely "to enable one to perform his duties as a good citizen." In 1970 everyone agreed that a statement was needed that would place a greater emphasis on the importance of education. How this was to be done and what was to be said would be a source of much controversy.

Seventeen member proposals on the objectives of education were presented to the convention.[4] Of these, six mentioned objectives as part of a broader proposal whereas eleven dealt directly with objectives. The general intent of these proposals was that the state

---

[4] Member Proposals 32, 72, 89, 90, 158, 167, 334, 347, 409, 434, 438, 439, 440, 441, 570. The text of these proposals is reproduced in Sixth Illinois Constitutional Convention, *Record of Proceedings,* 1970, Vol. VII.

should provide a high quality education for all (some proposals specified all children), regardless of race or religion, and that such education should include higher educational institutions as well as other institutions and services which might be desirable. Suggestions were also made that free education be provided to those with physical and mental handicaps. The intent of these provisions taken in general was quite broad: each child (or person) in the state was to be guaranteed a better and longer education. There were variations among the proposals: some would educate adults as well as children, some would provide a "high quality" rather than an "adequate" education, some would provide a "common school education" rather than one through the university level. These statements, basically hortatory, gave little indication of the coming controversy in the committee.

Almost all witnesses referred to the subject of educational objectives. Many merely affirmed the need for high quality education and then went on to other subjects. Few witnesses provided specific proposals. Some organizations, such as the Illinois Association of School Boards, recommended leaving section 1 as it was written in 1870, but questioning of these witnesses indicated that they would not be opposed to strengthening the section. As with the member proposals, there was little agreement as to the strength of the provision, length of schooling, or ages to be schooled, but neither did there seem to be much cause for controversy.

A DIVIDED COMMITTEE

Yet it was the topic of educational objectives that caused the most dissension among the members of the Committee on Education at the 1969–1970 convention. This was the subject that divided the members into the Young Turks and the Old Guard, and it was the committee's action upon this issue that caused the most public outcry. Elements of controversy existed, and could have reasonably been anticipated, because of the background of the committee members. The two black delegates, Patch and Pughsley, were obviously unhappy with the extremely inadequate education being offered to minority groups in the city of Chicago. Section 1 was their prime concern, for they felt it was in this section that high quality education and equal educational opportunity would be affirmed. The lawyers on the committee, Kamin, Dove, and Mathias, were aware of the hortatory nature of the section, and their professional training might logically have led them to seek a statement of goals which was as concise and simple as possible. The educators, Parker, Buford, Bottino, and to some extent Fogal, might have been expected to be more concerned with implementing specific educational goals. Evans and Howard, who had much experience in the League of Women Voters, might have opted to go along with the lawyers for a simple statement and with the educators for an implementation of certain specific proposals.

Thus, the lineup of forces for this discussion could have been Patch and Pughsley versus the rest of the committee. If this had been the case there would have been no controversy, since two delegates would not have constituted enough for a minority report. In the discussion of interaction of personalities, however, an analysis based upon predictable positions is often not adequate; this was true in the area of objectives as handled by the committee. The array of forces became one black (Pughsley was ill), two lawyers, one professor, and one League of Women Voters member versus one lawyer, three educators, and one member of the League of Women Voters. The basis of the division was obviously not background or exclusively professional training. Instead, the criteria were age, friendship, and, most importantly, ideas as to how much reform should be introduced into section 1.

Educational objectives did not appear unduly controversial at the inception of the discussions. The subject was taken up on February 25 after much debate had already taken place on structure. Discussion continued sporadically on March 3, 5, and 10; little progress was made but little dissension encountered. It was during this period that many of the younger members felt most discouraged about their hopes for the final outcome of the article, for they realized that the older members were not open to any large degree of innovation.

On March 5 the subcommittee on objectives (Buford, Patch, and Parker) presented its report:

> The well being of the State and its people requires that public

> education of high quality be provided and adequately supported
> to the end that each person may be educated to the limit of his
> ability.
>
> To achieve this goal, the State shall establish and support by
> law a system of free public schools.
>
> The State shall also establish such public institutions of higher
> learning and other educational services as are desirable.

The wording was accepted but not by a final vote, and Dr. Browne
was asked to begin to write the rationale that would accompany
the proposal on section 1. Each member had also prepared a statement of objectives for presentation. The proposals varied in length
from two lines by Dove to ten lines by Buford. Their content was
surprisingly similar: all mentioned other educational institutions
or institutions of higher learning, most mentioned providing a quality education, and almost all mentioned educating people or children to the limits of their capacities.

On March 10 Dr. Browne read what he had prepared, using the
subcommittee report and the various proposals from committee
members as a basis:

> The well-being of the State and its people requires that public
> education of high quality be provided and adequately supported
> to the end that each person may be educated to the extent of his
> ability.
>
> To achieve this goal, the State shall establish and support by
> law a system of free public schools and shall also establish such
> public institutions of higher learning and other educational ser-
> vices as are desirable.

The vote on acceptance of this language was seven to two in favor,
with Patch and Pughsley absent and Kamin and Dove voting no.
Since seven was a majority of the committee, it appeared this would
be the version of section 1 to be reported to the full convention.

After committee adjournment that day, however, Kamin, Dove,
and Howard discussed Dr. Browne's wording. Kamin and Dove
were particularly concerned over the use of the words "public education" and the word "schools." They feared these terms would be
read as a limitation on the scope of the state board of education,
barring extension of its authority to colleges and universities. Moreover, they were afraid that the term "public education" might be

thought to strengthen the prohibition in section 3 of aid to non-public schools, even if that section were left unchanged. On account of the terms "public education" and "free public schools," the courts might rule unconstitutional any programs, present or future, which would in some way give aid or support to nonpublic schools.

Howard was persuaded to join the other two delegates in their opposition to Dr. Browne's wording; the three wrote a new proposal which was shown to Patch, Fogal, and Bottino at the plenary session that day. When agreement among these six members was achieved, they did not show the new wording to any additional members of the committee because the six constituted a majority.

The following day the six members presented the new wording to the committee, stating that an ad hoc committee meeting had been held and the following formulated:

> It shall be the paramount duty of the State to provide a quality educational experience for all persons to the limits of their capacities.
>
> Toward this end, the State shall provide for a system of public educational institutions and services.

The minutes of March 11 record that Kamin stated, in explaining the new proposal, that there was little difference between it and the proposal approved the previous day, but that his understanding of the general feeling of the committee was that education should be approached as a whole. Therefore, no specific reference to public schools or to public education should be made which would in any way narrow the scope of education.

Parker was the first to respond to the new language, arguing that the section did not do what it should and that it omitted the word "free." Mathias also objected to this omission. Though this change was apparently made at Patch's suggestion,[5] it was primarily Kamin who defended it to the other members of the committee. He noted that many aspects of public education (such as textbooks and gyms and lockers) were not free and should not be implied to be so. In addition, the sponsors of the new wording considered the word

[5] According to Kamin, Patch, and Howard in interviews with the author, March 11, 1970.

"public" to be better than the word "free" where higher education and special services were concerned. Buford added his objections, but when a vote was taken the ad hoc committee had the necessary six votes for a majority. The remaining four members expressed their intention to write a minority report.

Although only two of the younger members had voted against Dr. Browne's wording, the other younger delegates had since been persuaded a better section was possible; they thought by banding together and including Bottino — who had agreed to their proposal — they would have sufficient numerical strength to determine the content of the majority report. The younger members originally felt, because of remarks that had been made by the older members in earlier informal committee discussions, that all would agree to the new proposal. However, the older members were unable to agree; they considered the statement too radical because it included the words "the paramount" and omitted the word "free." In addition, the older members objected to the way in which the matter had been handled. The creation of a new proposal after committee adjournment had not previously occurred, and the committee had always worked together or in recognized subcommittees. Also, there appeared to exist on the part of the older members a certain amount of distrust of the younger members, all of whom, except for Howard, were Democrats. This is shown most particularly by Parker's remark, "Why does Mayor Daley want that language?"[6]

Fears about the radical nature of the section and the omission of the word "free" caused Bottino to defect to the Old Guard side, thus creating a five-to-five stalemate in the committee and preventing either majority or minority reports from being written. Delegates on both sides realized that this matter, unlike the structural problems involved with creation of a state board of education, could not be passed on to the legislature. Because it involved broad policy decisions, it had to be resolved at the convention. When the committee became stalemated the Young Turks despaired of ever seeing their suggestions incorporated into the proposed article. Because of these feelings of futility the Young Turks created the game of opposing forces in the committee, pitting their desire for large reforms

---

[6] Interview with the author, March 11, 1970.

against the Old Guard's preference for more moderate change. The game gave the Young Turks a sense of satisfaction from being on a team and scheming against their opponents. The Old Guard also developed a group consciousness and was hesitant to vote with any members of the opposing team.

When informed by Patch that Pughsley was likely to return in the near future, the Young Turks were sure they would gain the majority. The game of opposing forces then became useful as a means to maintain the factions until Pughsley's return. As mentioned in Chapter I, the Young Turks had an additional incentive to delay: more sure of their solidarity than the Old Guard, they felt that a stalemate would eventually lead to a breakdown of unanimity among the older members. Team spirit was emphasized on both sides, and the factions remained for the time being steadfast in their positions.

On March 18 a new subcommittee on objectives was formed of delegates Buford, Parker, Dove, and Kamin. They attempted to reach a consensus, but on March 20 reported that the factions were still too divided to reach an agreement.

A Necessary Consensus

Developments both inside the committee and out were to change the inflexible positions of the two groups. News soon reached the committee about the public outcry over the omission of the word "free" from the Young Turks' section. The public feared that citizens would be forced to pay tuition for public school education unless they were guaranteed free education by the constitution.

This omission was given publicity by the news media, who were thirsting for information on Con-Con action. The most prominent emphasis was provided by Tony Abel of WCIA-TV in Champaign, a station that broadcasts to most of central and southern Illinois. The following is Abel's script from the evening of March 13:

> The omission of the word "free" from the wording in the new constitution's education article might well have been an oversight rather than an overt gesture on the part of the Education Committee — but even if that were not so, the decision at this point

is subject to many reviews. The Education Committee is split into two camps which might well be classified as a battle between the Old Guard and the Young Turks. Unfortunately, Old Guard committee chairman Paul Mathias of Bloomington found himself numbered among the minority when the vote came in.

The Young Turks have no formal leadership, but one of their more vocal members is Malcolm Kamin of Chicago's 12th district. Also identified with this faction is downstater Franklin Dove of Shelbyville, William Fogal of Pekin, Mrs. Betty Howard of St. Charles, Sam Patch of Chicago and others.

Their main attempt was to rewrite the committee's proposal so it would bind the state to public education as a "paramount" obligation. But, in their ambition, that fateful word "free" was also omitted, and the ire of so many was also raised.

If the Young Turks of the Education Committee do not over-react to public criticism, the wording might yet be changed to bring it more into line with public opinion.

No other committee at Con-Con is factionalized in such an apparent manner as the Education Committee. While the battle lines may be drawn on philosophical grounds, the borderlines of the two camps are surprisingly coincidental with age groups — lending some credence to observations that the skirmishes within the committee are in reality a kind of mature generation gap.

As Abel foresaw, public reaction to the omission was strong. People sought out their delegates and expressed their outrage, demanding that something be done. Letters of protest were written to the Committee on Education — forty-seven to Chairman Mathias alone — and most of the delegates received telegrams and telephone calls.

This public disapproval was to aid the delegates in reaching consensus, but another factor also became important. All members gradually became aware that a unanimous committee report would make the position of the group stronger when the report was presented to the full convention, thus increasing the likelihood that committee recommendations would be passed with little or no change. This realization eventually caused the members to attempt seriously to reach a consensus. With the outcry over the omission of "free," the Young Turks realized the necessity of quieting public opinion by reinserting the word into their proposal. They hoped that doing so would make the Old Guard more flexible in its position and that a compromise between the groups would be possible.

In late March Kamin proposed a new wording:

> The State shall provide for a system of universities, colleges, libraries, free common schools, and other such institutions of learning as may be deemed necessary.

The Old Guard was also moving closer to agreement, as is evidenced by this proposal from Buford:

> It shall be a paramount duty of the State to provide public education of high quality to the end that all persons can be educated to the limit of their capacities.
>
> Toward this end the State shall provide for a system of free public schools through the secondary level.
>
> It shall also provide for public institutions of higher learning and other educational services which may or may not be free.

On April 7 the committee was still unable to reach a consensus on several very similarly worded proposals. Distrust between the factions was high. The compromise wording presented by the Young Turks in March was rejected by the Old Guard. Then suddenly the Young Turk faction broke apart. Delegates Howard and Fogal, feeling that a unanimous report would not be possible, tiring of the endless debate, and stating that Buford's wording was at least acceptable, voted for that wording on April 7. Their action gave the Old Guard a seven-to-three majority.

All was to be changed the following day. Kamin and Dove were concerned that the words "public education" in Buford's proposal might lead by court interpretation to the prohibition of aid to non-public schools. In addition, Kamin said he feared the words "also could be used to limit the state's entry into other private areas such as support of the arts." After convincing Howard and Fogal of these possibilities, the Young Turks rewrote their proposed section. The words were mainly the work of Kamin, but the authorship purported to be that of Fogal, the quietest member of the young group and the one most trusted by the Old Guard.

On the morning of April 8 Fogal asked to be heard. He expressed great dismay over the divisiveness among the committee members and reminded them of the task ahead and of the importance of education. His presentation deeply moved the other members of the committee, and his new proposal met with immediate acceptance:

> The paramount goal of the people of the State shall be the educational development of all persons to the limits of their capacities.
>
> To achieve this goal, it shall be the duty of the State to provide for an efficient system of high quality public educational institutions and services.
>
> Education in the public schools at the primary and secondary levels shall be free. There shall be such other free education as the General Assembly may provide.

Minor revisions caused the last paragraph eventually to read: "Education in the public schools through the secondary level shall be free. There may be such other free education as the General Assembly provides."

Kamin and Patch asked to be recorded as agreeing to the above language "with reservations." In fact, this was part of the plan of the Young Turks to make the wording seem less a group effort and to make the situation more believable to the Old Guard. The atmosphere of togetherness created by this consensus permitted the resolution of most of the other issues before the committee on the same day.

Despite the realization of the benefits to be gained by consensus, the Young Turks viewed the compromise in terms of the game they had created; the agreement, they felt, had been attained on their terms, through Fogal's presentation which duped the opposite side. The consensus was to them, therefore, not a compromise but a victory. Their team won; the opponent was fooled; and the goal of extending the scope of education was accomplished. It is unlikely, however, that such a victory would have been possible had the Young Turks refused to change their position on the word "free." The change allowed the Old Guard to reconsider the wording of the Young Turks and to yield somewhat on their own position.

The final compromise, therefore, resulted from the division of the committee into factions, the need to appease the public, the desire to create a unanimous committee proposal, and Fogal's intermediary efforts. If Fogal had not voted for Buford's language on

April 7, it is unlikely the Old Guard would have voted for the new wording on April 8; it was Fogal's vote in favor of their proposal that caused the Old Guard to trust him. That trust, combined with Fogal's moving presentation and the committee's desire to write a unanimous report, was enough to lead the Old Guard to accept language they previously might have rejected.

The controversy over the degree of reform to be introduced into section 1 of the proposed education article was settled eventually by a compromise. The committee provided a strongly worded section guaranteeing free education at the elementary and secondary levels. The section contained the words "the paramount" (rather than "a paramount," upon which the Old Guard had been insisting) and on the whole extended the scope of education.[7] Development of the section had been incremental — a compromise between little change and radical innovation.

[7] That the section on objectives in the 1970 education article is being used to help extend the scope of education in Illinois is indicated by the following report from the Advisory Commission on Financing the Arts in Illinois:

> The framers of the new Constitution defined education broadly to include "expansion beyond the traditional public school programs" and to reach "all persons ... adults too ... to provide each person an opportunity to progress to the limit of his ability." Moreover, the framers expressly suggested that the educational enterprise reaches to "individuals ... whose cultural levels are lifted."
>
> Art has always been an element of sound education But the new Constitution is an expression of the State's obligation to support the arts beyond their inclusion in formal educational programs, to provide cultural opportunities to "all persons to the limits of their capacities."

Illinois, Advisory Commission on Financing the Arts in Illinois, *Report* (Chicago, 1971), p. 4.

IV

Providing for Higher Education

The Illinois Constitution of 1870 referred to higher education only in passing. Section 3 forbade payment of public funds to any college or university controlled by any church or sectarian denomination, but no other specific reference was made. Two resolutions regarding the establishment of a state university were presented to the delegates of the 1870 convention, but the Education Committee took no action on them. The attitude expressed in the 1870 debates toward institutions of higher learning was somewhat hostile.

More attention was given to the subject by the 1920 constitutional convention, where this section was included in the proposed constitution:

> "The general assembly shall make adequate provision for the maintenance and development of the University of Illinois and the system of state normal schools."

That constitution failed to be ratified by the voters, however, so by 1969 there were still no specific constitutional provisions in Illinois for education beyond the secondary level.

Thirteen member proposals presented to the 1969–1970 convention specifically addressed the subject of higher education. Almost half closely resembled Member Proposal 434:

> The General Assembly shall provide by law for a state-wide system of free public schools sufficient for the education of, and open to, all children of school age and shall provide for such

other public educational institutions as may be desirable for the intellectual, cultural and occupational development of the people of this State.

Three others were more strongly worded: Member Proposal 438 asked for the inclusion of a provision "guaranteeing the right of free quality education for all from pre-school through college." Member Proposal 439 suggested that the General Assembly provide for "the establishment and support of such other public educational services and institutions necessary for the fullest development of the intellectual, cultural and occupational potential of the people. It shall include all individuals from infancy through adulthood." Member Proposal 570 stated:

It is the policy of Illinois that no one will be denied the opportunity for an education beyond the secondary level solely because of financial need or other factors unrelated to ability.

One proposal, 334 from Delegate Mathias, was concerned solely with the subject of higher education:

The General Assembly shall establish and support such public institutions of higher learning as may be desirable.

These proposals all recognized the necessity for the state to make higher educational opportunities widely available.

The remaining proposals dealt with miscellaneous problems: Member Proposal 53 would have established a state board of education to govern education through the level of junior colleges and a board of higher education with jurisdiction over four-year colleges and graduate schools; Member Proposal 158 asked for the election of boards of trustees of state supported institutions of higher learning; Member Proposal 55 provided for at least one student member on the governing and coordinating bodies of state colleges and universities.

Most witnesses, other than those connected with higher education, did not speak directly on the subject of education beyond the secondary level. Of those who did, almost all gave testimony much like the recommendation from the Illinois Association of School Administrators:

The Legislature shall provide only for the support and maintenance of a system of free public schools guaranteeing equal educational opportunity and open to all children in the state and shall establish, organize, and support such other public educational institutions, including public institutions of higher learning, as may be desirable.

In 1870 the delegates had opposed providing higher education at public expense. By 1970 the need for longer educational preparation to live and work in today's world was apparent. Higher education was no longer regarded as a luxury by the general public, but a somewhat different attitude was found among the members of the Committee on Education. Although they recognized the place and need for higher education, the majority of the committee, especially the educators, felt this aspect of education had received undue attention and support at the expense of elementary and secondary education. Four members so indicated in response to a questionnaire:

Bottino: Greatest lobby in Illinois — receives financial support out of proportion to that of elementary–secondary schools.

Buford: I favored a single board of education for the state which in my judgment could give higher education the place it deserves in relationship to the total program of education.

[Responses elsewhere in Buford's questionnaire make it clear that higher education, in his estimation, "deserved" a lower priority in relationship to the total educational program.]

Dove: I developed a distaste and distrust for those apparently in command of higher education. This included legislators as well as administrators. I was amazed by the complexity of the administrative structure which appeared to me to be developed only for the purpose of protecting their special interest. . . . I believe that a State Board of Education if properly created by the legislature will destroy their Sacred Cow.

Howard: I feel that higher education has received a disproportionate amount of state finance.

Patch: The Board of Higher Education has too much influence and higher education has gotten a disproportionate share and has favored a certain class of people.

This hostile attitude does much to explain the array of forces for and against the concept of a superboard to govern all education. In the first vote on February 18, Buford, Dove, Fogal, Kamin, Howard, and Patch favored a superboard. Bottino, although somewhat antagonistic toward higher education, apparently thought the levels of education were sufficiently different to warrant two boards, as did delegate Parker. The Young Turks, especially, were concerned that education be treated as a whole, and expressed their views by supporting one board over all educational levels.

Additional hostility toward higher education was inadvertently created by Chairman Mathias. Because he was thought to have vested interests in higher education, any suggestion from him on education beyond the secondary level was met with distrust. Mathias — recognizing this hostility and upset by the results of the vote on the superboard — had gone to the Ad Hoc Advisory Committee on Con-Con of the Board of Higher Education, seeking support of his own Member Proposal 334. The Advisory Committee, led by Professor Gove and composed of representatives of the various higher education systems in Illinois, in turn went to the Board of Higher Education. The Board agreed to send representatives to the Committee on Education to speak in favor of the Mathias proposal. Their appearance on March 4, however, probably irritated rather than persuaded members of the committee; surprised by this unanticipated deluge of higher education spokesmen, they felt pressured by the chairman and became even more wary of the issue.

Among the witnesses was Dr. David Dodds Henry, president of the University of Illinois. Henry's appearance indicated that people in higher education deemed this issue very important to their interests. In fact, the University of Illinois had sent an observer to the convention to watch for any developments which might affect education beyond the secondary level. Robert Bentz, assistant to University vice-president Eldon Johnson, did not make himself conspicuous, and his presence and the reasons for it were unknown to most committee members as well as to most other delegates.

The witnesses spoke on two issues. They expressed their adamant opposition to the concept of a superboard, stating that higher education was enough different from elementary and secondary education to be governed by a separate board. Representatives of the

Board of Higher Education explained the need for the inclusion in the new constitution of Mathias's Member Proposal 334:

> The General Assembly shall establish and support such public institutions of higher learning as may be desirable.

The arguments of these witnesses were apparently persuasive enough to change slightly the positions of the committee members. A vote taken that same day showed five in favor of an overall board, four against, and one voting present. Kamin, who had previously voted in favor of a superboard, voted present. He had become concerned that the representatives of higher education would work to defeat the whole education article if it provided for a superboard.

In regard to the jurisdiction of the state board, the vote on February 18 had indicated no one was willing to leave that decision to the General Assembly. On March 4, however, Kamin, Evans, Mathias, and Bottino voted for just that option. As discussed in Chapter III, the issue of jurisdiction became entangled with the issue of educational objectives, which divided the committee into factions and created a great deal of ill will. It appears that because of the impending wrangle over the wording of educational objectives, the jurisdiction of the state board of education suddenly became a minor issue. The vote on March 5 was unanimous to leave the question to the legislature.

No one in committee again mentioned placing a specific reference to higher education in the constitution. Apparently too much hostility had been engendered, and Chairman Mathias recognized it. The Board of Higher Education also sensed the feelings of many members of the Committee on Education and decided not to ask that anything be included on this subject, fearing that any provision might be disadvantageous for higher education. In addition, they were concerned that the spring 1970 campus unrest and protests over the war in Vietnam might have caused a generally unfavorable attitude towards colleges and universities.

The old conflict over the amount of change in the education article reappeared during the discussion of higher education, although with different alignments. One side, led by Mathias, felt that constitutional recognition of higher education was necessary and attempted to have Member Proposal 334 included in the article. The other side feared that any change might give increased attention and support to higher education, so they opted for the status quo — no specific mention in the constitution. In the end, both sides were placated. Higher education was not specifically mentioned, but section 1 required the state "to provide for an efficient system of high quality public educational institutions and services." Even Mathias was pleased with this statement. In a letter written on September 28, 1971, he stated:

> It seems to me that the reference to "high quality public educational institutions" does include the colleges and universities. . . . I do not feel that detailed provisions with reference to higher education were necessary.[1]

For the committee one of the most fortunate aspects of the debate over higher education was that it created a new working relationship among the members. Though there was hostility, the realignment of forces put the Old Guard–Young Turk split into more reasonable perspective, and the committee saw that the two groups were not totally opposed to each other on all issues. The feeling of suspicion toward higher education among members of both groups helped provide a basis for resolution of the fight over the objectives of education.

[1] Letter from Paul Mathias to the author, dated September 28, 1971.

V

Aid to Nonpublic Schools:
Caution in the Face of Controversy

One of the most potentially controversial parts of the 1870 constitution was section 3 of the education article, Public Funds for Sectarian Purposes Forbidden:

> Neither the General Assembly nor any county, city, town, township, school district, or other public corporation, shall ever make any appropriation or pay from any public fund whatever, anything in aid of any church or sectarian purpose, or to help support or sustain any school, academy, seminary, college, university, or other literary or scientific institution, controlled by any church or sectarian denomination whatever; nor shall any grant or donation of land, money, or other personal property ever be made by the State, or any such public corporation, to any church, or for any sectarian purpose.

The issue was greatly feared by the delegates to the 1969–70 constitutional convention, in large part because of its impact on an attempt at constitutional revision in New York. There, the proposed constitution of 1967 replaced a ban on aid to nonpublic schools with the words of the First Amendment of the federal Constitution. In the opinion of many experts, the controversy that arose over that substitution was one of the main reasons for the defeat of the entire constitution.

The proponents and opponents of aid to nonpublic schools in Illinois were many and vocal. In September 1969 there were 2,773,029 students attending elementary and secondary schools in Illinois. Of these, 448,513, or approximately 20 percent of the students, attended nonpublic schools, most of which were run by the Catholic Church.[1] Many of these schools were being forced to close, purportedly because of lack of money and rising costs. According to proponents of aid, Catholic parents who had willingly supported parochial schools over the years could no longer keep up with rising tuition costs and increasing taxes. They were being forced to pay a "double taxation" — to support their own schools and to pay taxes for the support of public schools. (In Illinois over half of all property taxes went to the public schools, as did about half of the sales tax and a large part of the new income tax.) Those favoring aid also pointed out the increased cost to the public schools if nonpublic schools were to be forced to close. A publication of the Illinois Catholic Conference explained:

> If these 450,000 pupils were enrolled in public schools, the cost to taxpayers would be at least $210,600,000 based on the present minimum expenditure of $520.00 required for every pupil in average daily attendance.... The cost to taxpayers could be as much as $324,000,000 based on the Statewide average expenditure of approximately $800.00 per public school pupil in average daily attendance.[2]

The proponents of aid pointed out the dilemma faced by Catholic parents. If they sent their children to parochial schools they had to bear the increasingly burdensome double taxation. This they could avoid only by public school education which taught a kind of secular humanism to which they did not want their children exposed.

The opponents of aid based their opposition on a variety of reasons: the scarcity of funds available to the public schools, the necessity for maintaining the separation of church and state, the "hidden

---

[1] The accuracy of these figures, which are from the office of the Superintendent of Public Instruction of Illinois, has been questioned; however, they are the ones which the committee used. For a discussion of accurate figures, see Donald A. Erickson, *Crisis in Illinois Nonpublic Schools* (Springfield: State of Illinois, 1971), pp. A4–A8.

[2] *Facts and Figures About Nonpublic Schools in Illinois* (Chicago, 1970), p. 2.

wealth" of the Catholic Church, the concept of private education as a privilege and not a right, and the divisiveness in society which might result from such aid.

HISTORICAL BACKGROUND

Since this was the most controversial issue with which the committee dealt, a more detailed examination of its background is warranted. The early history of Illinois education contains many examples of the intermingling of religion, education, and the state. Although the legislature was reluctant to charter specifically denominational colleges, many academies, the most popular form of secondary school from 1825 to 1850, were granted charters. The charters usually stated that no religious discrimination was to be allowed, but these schools were founded and staffed by ministers of the various faiths, and the competition between the academies often reflected bitter sectarian rivalries.[3] The academies were not secular in the modern sense, for it was often stipulated that the Bible must be taught and the Christian religion encouraged. Indeed, as many settlers in Illinois came from older states of the east, they were, in the words of Justice Felix Frankfurter, merely following the tradition that "education of children was primarily study of the Word and the ways of God."[4] To the founders of these institutions and apparently also to the members of the General Assembly, nonsectarianism meant Protestant Christianity, which did not prohibit Bible reading or prayers. It was this interpretation of the meaning of nonsectarianism which was to make it difficult for the Catholics to accept the developing public school system.

During these controversies over religion in the public schools, the Illinois Constitutional Convention of 1870 was called. Two topics with which the convention was concerned were aid to nonpublic schools and Bible reading in public schools. These two issues were inextricably linked. Many citizens hoped that the public schools would Americanize the Catholic immigrant. Therefore, Protestant

---

[3] Daniel W. Kucera, *Church-State Relationships in Education in Illinois* (Washington, D.C.: The Catholic University of America Press, 1955), p. 29.
[4] Dissenting in *Illinois ex rel. McCullom v. Board of Education,* 333 U. S. 203 (1948), p. 213.

values had to be stressed in public schools, and parochial schools were not to be aided or encouraged. Catholic schools were seen as a foreign influence, for in addition to having an alien religious atmosphere, they were usually conducted in the native language of the immigrant.[5] Lyman Beecher, one of the most influential Protestant clergymen of the period, stated:

> Let the Catholics mingle with us as Americans, and come with their children under the full action of our common schools and republican institutions, and the various powers of assimilation, and we are prepared cheerfully to abide the consequences.[6]

And again:

> Can Jesuits and nuns, educated in Europe, and sustained by patronage of Catholic powers in arduous conflict for the destruction of liberty be safely trusted to form the mind and opinions of the young hopes of this nation? Is it not treason to commit the formation of republican children to such influences?[7]

Catholic criticism of sectarianism in public schools was looked upon as "a veritable threat or peril to the very existence of the public school, the *sine qua non* for the continuing stability of the American social order."[8]

The ban on aid to nonpublic schools which emerged from the 1870 convention as section 3 of Article VIII is especially significant in that it was the first really "strict" constitutional prohibition on this subject written by any state.[9] The debates show that in estab-

---

[5] J. A. Burns, *The Growth and Development of the Catholic School System in the United States* (New York: Benziger Brothers, 1912), pp. 299–336. In 1906 the membership of Catholic parishes speaking foreign languages was as follows: German, 1,519,978; Italian, 826,023; French, 1,031,530; Polish, 736,150; Slovak, 78,353; Portuguese, 48,227; Hungarian, 26,472.

[6] Lyman Beecher, *A Plea for the West* (Cincinnati: Truman & Smith, 1835), p. 60.

[7] Ibid., p. 105.

[8] Peter DeBoer, "A History of Early Compulsory School Attendance Legislation in the State of Illinois" (Ph.D. diss., University of Chicago, 1968), pp. 526–27.

[9] For present purposes a strict ban is defined as one which (a) specifically precludes "direct or indirect benefits," (b) forbids aid for "any sectarian purpose," (c) forbids use of not only the common school fund but any "public money, land, appropriation, gift or grant of any kind," and (d) states everything in considerable detail. A loose ban is characterized as one which (a) is

lishing this provision the delegates apparently were not responding to any specific situation in Illinois, but rather to a fear as to possible future difficulties:

> It is true that up to this time we have suffered little inconvenience from the want of such a provision. But as Sects grow up in this state, unless we have some check, the time is not far distant when we will find them pressing upon the Legislature, and so managing the school funds as to make them subservient to building up their peculiar religious opinions.

Statements were made about the situation in New York, where Catholics had attempted to gain a share of the public school funds, and it was pointed out that this must not be allowed to happen in Illinois. Two significant amendments were introduced, one of which would have allowed some aid to nonpublic schools and the other of which would have reimbursed parents who could not in good conscience send their children to the public schools; both amendments were soundly defeated.

Important to note is the lack of opposition among the delegates to the final provision. Most of the debate centered on how the ban should be worded, not whether it should be included. Significant also is the fact that there were no Catholics among the delegates to the 1870 convention, and it is interesting to speculate on whether the provision would have been different had Catholics been represented.

The 1870 debate on aid to nonpublic schools was notable for its lack of name calling and emotion. The delegates were careful to point out that they held no animosity for Catholics or for the Catholic Church. Very different, however, was the debate on the issue of Bible reading in the public schools. The Committee on Education

very short and nondetailed, *or* (b) mentions only aid from the common school fund *or* (c) prohibits aid to sectarian schools only, rather than for "any sectarian purpose," *or* (d) does not explicitly forbid indirect as well as direct benefits, *or* (e) exhibits more than one of these characteristics.

In terms of these criteria, thirty-one states had loose bans as of the writing of the 1970 Illinois Constitution, thirteen had strict bans, four had references that fell somewhere between loose and strict, and two had no mention of aid to nonpublic schools at all. Jane Galloway Buresh, "Educational Issues at the 1969–1970 Illinois State Constitutional Convention" (Ph.D. diss., University of Chicago, 1972), p. 136.

included no mention of the subject in its report, but the following proposal was offered from the floor:

> The General Assembly shall pass such laws as will effectually prevent school officers, or any person or persons having control of the common schools of the State, from excluding the Bible from said schools.

Many petitions had been presented to the delegates from individuals and organizations desirous of Bible reading in the public schools. The debate centered around Catholic-Protestant differences, since the main difficulty was the Catholics' objection to the King James version of the Bible. Nativist arguments and name calling were rampant. A Mr. Bayne declared:

> Europe is pouring her population upon us by the thousands every year. . . . This vast influx of population know but little about the fundamental principle either of civil government or Christianity. With that amount of ignorance and superstition coming in upon us, I say it is well for every American freeman to look well to the principle upon which civil government rests.

A Mr. Gamble concurred and stated:

> Said a Romish priest, when commenting upon the losses of the Romish church in Italy: "We can afford to let the rags of Italy go into the hands of Garibaldi, when we are taking possession of the United States." . . . At a meeting of Roman Catholics held in New York last year . . . one of the speakers, exulting over what had been gained by them through appropriations from the New York Legislature said, "this is the little finger, and we must preserve it until we get the whole hand."

Though there were no Catholic delegates, many non-Catholics disavowed the proposal, saying it was a violation of the rights of conscience. One said:

> Under a republican government we have no right to lord it over the consciences of others. The Catholics and Hebrews have, on the question of the Bible, their own convictions, and even if we believe these convictions to be less enlightened than our own, we must admit that the possessors of them are equally sincere.

After lengthy and heated debate, it was finally decided to omit the question of Bible reading from the constitution so as not to jeopardize its acceptance by the voters.

Although the inclusion of the ban on aid to nonpublic schools would seem almost exclusively a reaction to the New York situation, deeper investigation shows otherwise. The denial by the delegates of any antagonism toward the Catholic Church was undercut by the highly emotional debate surrounding the issue of Bible reading in the public schools.

These emotional, anti-Catholic feelings were not limited to Illinois; they intruded even on the national level. In an address in 1875 President Ulysses S. Grant stated:

> Encourage free schools and resolve that not one dollar appropriated for their support shall be appropriated to the support of any sectarian schools. . . . Leave the matter of religion to the family altar, the church, and the private schools supported entirely by private contributions. Keep the church and state forever separate.[10]

In his annual message to Congress in December 1874, Grant called for a constitutional amendment specifically prohibiting expenditure of public funds for direct or indirect aid to any religious sects. Such an amendment was sponsored by James C. Blaine, the Republican leader of the House of Representatives:

> No State shall make any law respecting an establishment of religion or prohibiting the free exercise thereof, and no money raised for the support of public schools, or derived from any public fund therefor, nor any public lands devoted thereto, shall ever be under the control of any religious sect, nor shall any money so raised or lands so devoted be divided between religious sects or denominations.[11]

This amendment passed the House by a vote of one hundred eighty to seven (ninety-eight not voting) but failed to receive the necessary two-thirds vote in the Senate. Between 1870 and 1888 eleven separate attempts had been made to secure an amendment prohibiting

[10] Quoted in John H. Lauback, *School Prayers — Congress, the Courts and the Public* (Washington, D.C.: Public Affairs Press, 1969), pp. 29–30.
[11] Quoted in ibid., p. 30.

aid to sectarian schools. The Blaine Amendment of 1876, however, was the only one to pass at least one house of Congress.

Was the debate over aid to nonpublic schools limited at the time to a handful of states, or was Illinois just one among many in which dissension was encountered? When constitutional provisions prohibiting aid to nonpublic schools are categorized as nonexistent, loose, medium, or strict, it becomes evident that all those termed strict were written after the Illinois ban.[12] Four states duplicated the Illinois provision almost exactly (Colorado, 1876; Idaho, 1899; Missouri, 1875; and Montana, 1889). Except for Illinois, all constitutional bans classified as strict were written at about the same time — during or soon after the Blaine Amendment controversy of 1875–1876. Many states adopted wording similar to that amendment. Three states had enacted some sort of ban in the 1840s, eight between 1850 and 1860, six from 1860–70, ten from 1870–80, seven from 1880–90, three from 1890–1900, and five more by 1918.

The issue, apparently much aggravated by the attempt of Catholics in New York to secure a portion of the public school funds and given national attention by the Blaine Amendment of 1876, finally began to recede during the 1920s; by that time all states but Maryland and Vermont had some sort of prohibition of aid to nonpublic schools. In the early 1920s Oregon tried to outlaw nonpublic schools altogether. The right of these schools to exist was then affirmed by the United States Supreme Court in *Pierce* v. *Society of Sisters* (268 U.S. 510, 1925).

The apparent lack of strictness in some constitutional provisions of the times may have been due to the desire for constitutional purity, or a feeling that one concise statement was sufficient to accomplish the purpose. All forty-six bans were written during a period of high anti-Catholic feeling (1840–1920). Catholic buildings could not be insured, unless constructed of non-flammable materials, because of the high risk of their being burned down.[13] The blatantly anti-Catholic Know Nothing party captured five state legislatures in 1855. Nativism was widely popular during the forties

12 See footnote 8, *supra.*
13 Anson Phelps Stokes and Leo Pfeffer, *Church and State in the United States* (New York: Harper & Row, 1964), p. 229.

and fifties. The "songster" of the American Republican Party, founded in 1843, reflects the spirit of the time:

> Then strike up "Hail Columbia!" boys, our free and happy land,
> We'll startle knavish partisans and break the Jesuit's band.
> We'll snap the reins, spurn party chains and priestly politics,
> We swear it by our father's [sic] graves — our sires of Seventy-six.[14]

Since the 1920s various constitutional conventions and amendments have dealt with aid to nonpublic schools. The proposed Illinois Constitution of 1922 omitted the ban on aid completely. Alaska and Hawaii, writing constitutions in the 1950s, did not include strict bans; Alaska's delegates specifically prohibited only "direct" aid. In 1947 New Jersey completely removed her prohibition of aid to nonpublic schools. In 1968 Florida significantly weakened her 1885 ban. Maryland did not attempt to insert such a restriction into her constitution during her recent convention. Rhode Island left her bans as originally written.

The controversy surrounding the subject of aid to nonpublic schools, however, was not dead when the Sixth Illinois Constitutional Convention convened. The conflict engendered by New York's attempt to reword its ban was discussed at the outset of this chapter. Nor have feelings on the subject entirely cooled since Illinois's convention. As recently as November 1970, the issue was again brought to public attention when Michigan voters adopted an amendment to their constitution which was much more strongly worded than their original section. That amendment specifically barred the state from providing transportation for children in non-public schools and apparently outlawed most other auxiliary services, including shared time.[15]

---

[14] Cited in ibid., p. 233.

[15] However, in a decision on March 31, 1971 *(Traverse City School District v. Attorney General,* 384 Mich. 390, 185 N.W. 2d 9), the Michigan Supreme Court struck down the following clause as unconstitutional: "No payment, credit, tax benefit, exemption or deduction, tuition, voucher, subsidy, grant or loan of public moneys or property shall be provided, directly or indirectly, to support the attendance of any student or employment of any person at any such non-public school or at any location or institution where instruction is offered in whole or in part to such non-public school students." Consequently, according to the interpretation of Prof. Donald Erickson of the University of Chicago, the language of the amendment is misleading, for the courts have

It is obvious that prejudice against Catholics was one of the main reasons for the creation of the constitutional bans on aid to nonpublic schools in various states. Although financial reasons have since been given for retaining or strengthening these prohibitions, the emotion surrounding the issue when it has arisen could lead one to wonder whether the real reasons were being stated.

Hearing Out the Opposing Sides

Eleven member proposals on aid to nonpublic schools were presented to the Sixth Illinois Constitutional Convention. Of these, four could be termed against aid while seven could be categorized as for aid to nonpublic schools. Of those against, Member Proposal 204 recommended retention of section 3 of Article VIII and Proposals 53, 90, and 158 suggested a rewording of the existing section (for instance, Member Proposal 90 recommended the sentence, "No public funds shall be used for sectarian education."). Of the seven proposals favoring aid, Numbers 101, 152, 192, and 544 asked for complete repeal of the existing section. Member Proposal 91 suggested allowing a tax credit or deduction for the parents of children in nonpublic schools. Member Proposal 253 recommended that a sentence be added to the 1870 section that such section does not preclude any form of aid to education that is permissible under the United States Constitution. Member Proposal 285 asked that nonpublic schools or the parents of children attending such schools be eligible for reimbursement for the value of nonreligious education.

More witnesses spoke specifically on the subject of aid to nonpublic schools than on any other issue before the Committee on Education and, very likely, than on any other issue before the convention. Almost 75 percent of those people testifying during public hearings in Wheaton and Chicago spoke on aid to nonpublic schools. Two separate meetings were held with the Bill of Rights Committee to hear experts on both sides of the question. It was found that most educational organizations and experts who

held that shared time is clearly valid on public premises and valid in some instances on nonpublic school premises as well. Erickson and George F. Madaus, "The Michigan Story: The Effects of Extending and Withdrawing Parochiaid," in United States, President's Commission on School Finance, *Issues of Aid to Nonpublic Schools* (Washington, D.C., 1971), p. 33.

testified before either the Education Committee alone or the joint committees were opposed to any form of aid. Such groups included the Illinois Education Association, the Illinois Congress of Parents and Teachers, the Superintendents Round Table of Northern Illinois, the Citizens Schools Committee, the Illinois Association of School Administrators, the Independent Voters of Illinois, and the Illinois State Chamber of Commerce.

There were, however, some surprises. Both the incumbent state superintendent of public instruction, Ray Page, and the Democratic candidate for that office, Dr. Michael Bakalis, indicated support for aid to nonpublic schools, as did Chicago Superintendent of Schools James Redmond and the Welfare Council of Metropolitan Chicago. Two other influential organizations, the League of Women Voters and the Illinois Federation of Teachers, chose to take no position on the issue.

In total, forty-one witnesses testified before the Committee on Education against aid to nonpublic schools and thirty-five witnesses spoke in favor of aid. Most witnesses on both sides were representatives of religious groups. The majority of Catholics spoke in favor of aid, although there were two exceptions who felt the church had enough money to support its own schools. Almost all representatives of Protestant groups opposed aid. A notable exception was Thomas Hubbard, of the Presbyterian Settlement House on the western side of Chicago, who spoke in support of the concept, saying that if private schools were to close, older neighborhoods would lose their stability since many residents would leave. The Christian Action Ministry also favored aid. Among the non-Catholic groups opposed to aid were the Metropolitan Chicago Baptist Association, the Illinois Council of Churches, the Ethical Humanist Society of Chicago, the Jewish War Veterans of the U.S.A., representatives of the Third Unitarian Church of Chicago, and a representative of the Seventh Day Adventist Church.

Two legal experts spoke to the committee on the subject of aid to nonpublic schools. Jordan Jay Hillman, professor of law at Northwestern University, asked for the retention of Article VIII, section 3, because he feared any change in the section might result in the defeat of the proposed constitution by the voters. It was Hillman's opinion that the Illinois ban on aid to nonpublic schools was less restrictive than the federal First Amendment. Various court decisions made under the Illinois prohibition, such as *Dunn v. Chicago Industrial School for Girls* (280 Ill. 613, 1917), permitted the state to pay to sectarian institutions at least part of the cost of caring for dependent children committed to them by the state. Prof. Philip B. Kurland of the University of Chicago Law School similarly indicated that the language of section 3 was probably no more restrictive than the federal language and would yield the same substantive results. Although Kurland made no recommendation on the committee's action regarding section 3, the members used his testimony as the basis for the rationale that accompanied their proposal to retain the section.

By far the two most vociferous groups testifying on the issue were Protestants and Other Americans United for Separation of Church and State, which opposed aid, and Citizens for Educational Freedom, which favored aid. These two groups had also been involved in the controversy over aid to nonpublic schools in New York in 1967, and although by the time of the Illinois convention they had somewhat tempered their remarks, they still issued misinformation on the subject. For example, in a bulletin Protestants and Other Americans United stated:

> This one church is worth at least 80 billion dollars, and has an annual income of at least thirteen billion. One order, the Jesuits, owns the Bank of America, has a controlling interest in the Phillips Petroleum Company, and is one of the largest stockholders in the Republic and National Steel companies. Also they are among the most important owners of the four greatest aircraft manufacturing companies in the United States — Boeing, Lockheed, Douglas and Curtiss-Wright. (Send for books and documents on this.) [16]

Fortunately, most of the testimony presented on the issue was not of this nature. In general the arguments, both pro and con, fell into five categories: the wall of separation, the child benefit theory, the public function of nonpublic schools, the integrative versus divisive effect, and financial considerations.

---

[16] Protestants and Other Americans United for the Separation of Church and State, *Before Jeopardizing the Future* (Chicago, 1970), p. 2.

Those witnesses against aid stated that the concept of separation of church and state has always been a part of the federal legal tradition. They said freedom of religion, as guaranteed by the First Amendment to the federal Constitution, is possible only if religious groups are free to function in their sphere of activity without interference or support from government. If public assistance were given to church schools, these witnesses contended, the government would have to determine which schools qualify for such aid, thus placing the government in the position of defining a legitimate religion and of supervising the curriculum and instruction of religious schools. This was said to destroy the principle of religious freedom under which religious schools operate.

To the proponents of aid the argument based on the separation of church and state as applied to aid was false; they believed the separation required by the federal Constitution was the separation necessary to promote religious liberties. To bar the child from receiving aid for secular subjects because of the presence of religion in a school was to them discrimination based on religion, not neutral action by the state.

The second argument was the child benefit theory, which — as used by the Supreme Court in *Board of Education* v. *Allen* (392 U.S. 236, 1968) — sees certain services as benefiting the child and not the institution. Those favoring aid explained that the purpose of aid to a private school is not to benefit the institution but to provide the child with an equal opportunity for an adequate education despite religious belief. The religion of a child is not subject to control by the state, but the child himself is subject to its control. If the child may fulfill his duty to the state by attending a parochial school, the state should be able to fulfill its duty to the child by facilitating his attendance. Those opposed to aid called it impossible to benefit the child without benefiting the institution. Parents who enjoy the freedom of choice of private schools must, they said, assume full obligation for the support of these schools. They contended the child is not denied free instruction in secular subjects, since that is available in the public schools.

A third argument on this issue was whether or not nonpublic schools served a sufficient public function to receive aid. Those favoring aid stated that the public purpose of compulsory school attendance laws is equally achieved whether the child is educated in a state or an independent school. Hence, there should be no penalty and no denial of educational tax funds if parents exercise their civil rights in the choice of an independent school. Since education has been termed an investment in human capital, they said, it is inconsistent with sound economic practice for governments to discriminate against the nonpublic school pupil and invest only in the public school student. They argued that without aid many private schools would not be able to perform at a high level and thus would produce citizens without a first-rate education.

Those against aid claimed that private schools have the privilege of defining their activities and their clientele and are legally responsible only to their own membership, whereas public schools have the privilege of receiving tax support but must serve and be responsible to the whole community. In addition, nonpublic schools often embrace objectives which are not legitimate public purposes, such as inculcating religious beliefs, giving a superior education to the wealthy, insuring the continuity of class characteristics, and avoiding the integration of the races.

These last points are closely related to the fourth argument — the integrative versus divisive effect of nonpublic school education. Those against aid seemed to feel that private and parochial schools encourage a divisiveness at a stage in a child's development when he should be learning to mingle with people unlike himself. Assignment of public funds to nonpublic schools could, they felt, easily lead additional religious, social, economic, or racial groups to undertake full-scale parochial or private education which, in turn, would lead to further divisiveness in society and to an erosion of the public school system. One of the most prevalent arguments was that the support of private education would lead to a greater amount of segregation of the races. In the South many state plans to support private education had been declared unconstitutional on the grounds that they were designed to establish and maintain a system of segregated schools.[17]

To counter this argument those favoring aid pointed to the func-

[17] See, for example, *Poindexter* v. *Louisiana Financial Assistance Commission*, 296 F. Supp 686 (E. D. La.), *aff'd sub. nom. Louisiana Commission for Needy Children* v. *Poindexter*, 393 U. S. 17 (1968).

tion nonpublic schools serve in providing alternative approaches in a pluralistic society. Children who are educated in different environments are more likely to become thinking, creative citizens, they argued, when confronted with viewpoints different from their own. They rejected any contention that the good of American society is identical or coextensive with the good of the public schools.

Perhaps the most frequent argument heard on both sides, especially among lay citizens, was the financial argument. Proponents of aid, of course, pointed to the lack of money to keep nonpublic schools running, to the fact that parents of children attending these schools were forced to pay a double taxation, and to the huge increase in expenditure the closing of nonpublic schools would cause the taxpayer. The opponents of aid stressed that there were insufficient funds available to support even the public schools, that if parents chose private education they should support it financially, and that the increased cost to taxpayers if all nonpublic schools were to close would be much less than the cost of aid given to such schools.

Surprising Unanimity on a Difficult Question

The large amount of research asked for by the committee on this subject indicates the apprehension felt by the members. Early in the convention the committee had been informed of the experts' opinions on the cause of the defeat of the proposed New York State Constitution of 1967. The committee was in agreement that aid to nonpublic schools should be one of the last issues it would deal with so outside hostilities would not be awakened to influence the consideration of other matters.

Although witnesses had testified on aid to nonpublic schools and delegates had presented their proposals on the subject, there was no formal committee discussion on the issue prior to March 19. A tentative hand vote taken on March 4 showed that seven members were in favor of retaining section 3 as it was written, three were disposed to make it stronger, and one voted to remove the section completely. The three who wished to strengthen section 3 were Dove, Fogal, and Patch. Howard, from a largely Catholic area, voted for deletion. Dove said early in the convention he "had not realized the emotional nature of this issue." Although his daughter attended a parochial school, Patch objected to the role such schools played in the city: "Many whites send their children to these schools so as to avoid the heavy black concentration in the public schools."[18] Again it should be noted that of the committee members only Bottino was a Catholic.

When formal discussion in committee began on March 19 it was generally agreed that the subject must not be allowed to get out of hand and thereby endanger the whole document. Even though separate submission of the section on aid was still a possibility, that alone would not have eliminated the potentially divisive controversy which could endanger the entire constitution's chance for passage. On March 25 an informal survey of the delegates showed the following positions on section 3: Bottino, Dove, Evans, and Kamin: retain; Buford: retain or strengthen; Mathias: retain or insert the language of the First Amendment. Fogal and Patch would have preferred to strengthen the section but would accept retention. Howard preferred deletion but retention was acceptable to her also. Parker felt strengthening the section would be wiser but retention was acceptable.

It is clear that the delegates were moving toward a decision to keep Article VIII, section 3, as written in 1870. Mathias was absent for the final vote on April 8 and Patch passed, but all others voted in favor of retention. The outcome was no surprise; the rationale to accompany the committee proposal had been written prior to the vote and was approved, with a few changes, on April 9.[19]

Two significant factors had contributed to this decision: first, the fear and emotion surrounding the issue made the committee members hesitant to recommend even the slightest change. Second, although many witnesses would have much preferred to see the section either deleted or significantly strengthened, the overwhelming majority, including very influential organizations on both sides of the issue, specifically asked for retention. Among those so doing

[18] Interview with the author, March 25, 1970.

[19] In fact, the committee counsel had been assured from the outset that section 3 would be retained without change. When approached in January to serve as counsel, Dr. Browne had demurred; since he was on record as opposing any change in section 3, he felt he would be embarrassed to be associated with a committee which proposed such change. Mathias and Buford assured him at that time that no change in section 3 could possibly come from the committee.

who opposed aid were the Illinois Congress of Parents and Teachers and the Illinois Education Association. On the other side, the most influential organization favoring aid, the Illinois Catholic Conference, also asked that section 3 be retained. This organization was presenting the official position of the Catholic Church on the issue. That organizations with such opposed viewpoints should recommend the same alternative revealed both the confusing effect of court interpretation of section 3 and the sophistication of the Catholic lobbyists, who obviously were familiar with those court interpretations.

The committee was faced with five alternatives. The first possibility, to strengthen section 3, was unacceptable to the committee. It would have created great opposition from those in favor of aid. Its effect might have been to invalidate such existing programs as the Illinois State Scholarship program, the school lunch program, aid to handicapped children, and pupil transportation. In addition, as the committee stated in its report, "More restrictive language . . . might entirely prohibit the State from doing business with any private entity." The committee had "no desire to retard or eliminate such established programs, nor to venture into unexamined areas of restriction where the effects could go far beyond education."

The remaining four alternatives were to retain the 1870 language, to weaken the 1870 section, to substitute the wording of the First Amendment prohibiting any law "respecting an establishment of religion," or to strike the entire section. The committee followed the reasoning of the legal experts in rejecting the last three alternatives. To change the 1870 language to one of these alternatives would make a difference only if the alternatives were more permissive than section 3. The committee realized that no provision should be adopted that would be more permissive than the First Amendment language because it would be struck down by the federal courts. The committee was of the opinion that, in fact, Illinois Supreme Court interpretations of the 1870 wording had about the same practical effect as the Supreme Court's interpretation of the First Amendment of the federal Constitution. In addition, legal opinion held that section 3 was no more restrictive than the federal language, and yielded the same substantive results.[20] Therefore,

[20] On the impact of retaining or revising section 3, see Braden and Cohn, pp. 404–09.

the committee reasoned, if any of the last four alternatives would yield the same result, why change the 1870 language at all, especially when any change would only arouse the opposition of one group or another?

All religious and educational organizations seemed well satisfied with retaining section 3 as it read, even though they were or should have been cognizant of the aid which might be allowed under this section. Thus, the committee determined to make no change in the existing language; that is, they instructed Style and Drafting to retain the section exactly as written in 1870, without even the changes in punctuation that might have been made as a technical matter.

If this issue had not been so controversial and if the delegates had not known from New York's experience of the effects of the removal of the ban on aid, the same degree of conflict might well have developed over change in this section as was exhibited regarding other sections of the education article. The lawyers on the committee, familiar with court interpretations of the issue, might have fought for deletion of the section or the insertion of the wording of the First Amendment. The educators, fearing what aid to nonpublic schools would do to the public schools, might have insisted the section be strengthened. However, the apprehension felt by all members, the fear of bringing the issue to the floor without the strength of a unanimous committee position, and the necessity to calm vocal public opinion caused all members to agree to retention of Article VIII, section 3.

VI

The Financing of Education:
Beginning to Face a Long-Range Problem

The last of the five major issues to be considered by the Committee on Education was the financing of the public school system in Illinois. The matter was taken up after submission of the committee's first report to the convention, and was ultimately submitted as a second report. No previous Illinois constitutional convention had dealt with this subject, perhaps because past delegates had seen it as a matter for legislative determination.[1]

During the school year 1968–1969 the cost of operating the schools in Illinois was approximately two billion dollars.[2] Although Illinois ranked fairly high among the states in total expenditure per pupil ($973 average), only a small amount of this total, 27 percent, came from state funds. An increase in the guaranteed minimum support (from $400 per pupil in average daily attendance to the $520 provided by the 1969 General Assembly)[3] had actually raised the support level to over 30 percent by the time of the convention.

---

[1] It is important to remember that this issue was being considered before the California decision in *Serrano* v. *Priest* (5 Cal. 3rd 584, 487 P.2d 1241, 96 Cal. Rptr. 601, 1971) and the Texas decision in *Rodriguez* v. *San Antonio Independent School District* (357 F. Supp. 280 (W. D. Texas, 1972)). For a discussion of the impact of these cases on constitutionality of school financing systems, see Chapter IX, *infra*.

[2] These and other figures cited are from the Office of the Superintendent of Public Instruction of Illinois.

[3] The foundation figure was determined as follows:

(a) Average daily attendance of pupils was weighted, with each elementary

However, the delegates were working with figures given to them prior to this increase.

Even with 30 percent of the money for public school education provided by state funds, approximately 64 percent still had to be supplied by local financing, the remaining 6 percent coming from federal grants and small miscellaneous sources such as the income from school lands. At the time of the convention the funds for public education through the secondary level came chiefly from locally levied property taxes. Over three-fifths of the resources for operating expenses and almost all of the funds for capital expenditures were supplied by these taxes.

The method of financing based mainly on property taxes has caused vast inequalities in the money spent on education from district to district. Since property is not distributed equally throughout the state and since school district lines are drawn without regard to assessed valuation, the amount of tax money available to such districts varies.[4] Some communities have a disproportionately small share of school responsibilities. Table 1 shows the large differences in assessed valuation as of 1969.

Thus a school district with only $5,462 of assessed valuation per pupil would need to levy a 4 percent educational tax to yield as much as $210 per pupil, which is far below the present cost of minimal schooling. Another district with $105,815 of assessed valuation would produce the amount of about $4,230 per pupil at a 4 percent rate, which is more than is probably needed for even the highest quality education. In one elementary district a 4 percent rate would produce more than $14,000 per pupil. Thus the amount

pupil given the value of 1.0, each kindergarten pupil 0.5, and each high school pupil 1.25.

(b) The qualifying tax rate for unit districts was $1.08 per $100 of assessed valuation and $0.90 for dual districts. If these tax rates failed to equal the equalization level of $520 per weighted pupil in average daily attendance (1969 level), the state paid the difference. This had the effect of guaranteeing funds to provide a "foundation level" in each district.

(c) In any case, the state would provide a "flat grant" of at least $48 per weighted pupil in average daily attendance.

[4] Assessed valuation is defined by the Office of the Superintendent of Public Instruction as "a valuation determined by a governmental unit upon real and personal property which provides a basis for levying taxes." Assessed valuation per pupil is therefore the total assessment for a school district divided by the number of pupils in that district.

TABLE I. ASSESSED VALUATIONS PER AVERAGE DAILY ATTENDANCE PUPIL

	Highest	*Median*	*Lowest*
Unit Districts			
Over 12,000 pupils	$23,733	$18,421	$10,452
6,000–12,000 pupils	24,501	17,711	11,024
3,000–6,000 pupils	31,292	18,575	7,127
1,000–3,000 pupils	99,086	18,732	8,474
Under 1,000 pupils	54,494	26,947	6,662
Elementary Districts			
Over 6,000 pupils	39,354	24,720	10,286
3,000–6,000 pupils	54,972	22,970	7,629
1,000–3,000 pupils	65,660	20,634	6,450
Under 1,000 pupils	372,160	29,822	5,462
High School Districts			
Over 6,000 pupils	87,978	53,309	42,977
3,000–6,000 pupils	105,815	55,588	27,524
1,000–3,000 pupils	88,713	53,137	24,118
Under 1,000 pupils	235,611	70,172	26,197

NOTE: Compiled from Illinois Education Association, *Educational Effort Study* (Springfield, 1970).

of money spent on education for a child in an Illinois school is largely a product of where that particular student resides. In poorer districts, which can least afford a high tax rate, the citizens must place a heavy tax burden on themselves in order to achieve the same level of spending that is reached by wealthier districts through a light tax load.

EMERGING CONCERN IN COMMITTEE

For decades Illinois has sought to overcome these inequalities through a foundation level program as established by the legislature.[5] At the time of the convention, however, Illinois ranked only thirty-fourth among states in state support for education. Many delegates felt that the only way to overcome present educational inequalities was to institute a system of full state funding of the common schools. Such a position was reflected in Member Proposal 434:

[5] See note 3, *supra*.

Funds for the public schools shall be appropriated by the General Assembly and no local governmental unit may levy taxes or appropriate funds for educational purposes.[6]

Member Proposal 32 stated, in the same vein:

No school district may levy a property tax for educational purposes as distinguished from building purposes.

Although many delegates were opposed to consideration of this matter altogether, still others, while feeling that total state financing was too extreme an approach, did favor the more moderate measures typified by Member Proposal 570:

The State has the primary duty to finance the public school system. The State may provide for the establishment of local school districts as it deems necessary for purposes of administration and operation, or financing, or both.

Most witnesses who spoke to the committee at least alluded to the subject of financing the public school system, although some merely stressed the need for increased funds. Many emphasized the need for true "equal educational opportunity," and others asked that a source other than local property taxation be found to support schools. Professional educators especially stressed the need for the removal of the five percent limit on bonded indebtedness; this matter was not, however, under consideration by the Education Committee.

Experts on financing were invited to speak to the committee; discussion began in mid-April and continued through May, June, and part of July. The witnesses included representatives from the Illinois Association of School Boards, the Chicago Board of Education, the Illinois School Building Commission, the Statistical Information Department of the Office of the Superintendent of Public Instruction, the Illinois Education Association, the Bureau of the Budget, and the Board of Higher Education. A general "think tank" meeting was held with various educational experts on May 12, and the experts were asked to mail in suggested constitutional

[6] This proposal was sponsored by Kamin. He introduced it, however, at the urging of the Welfare Council of Metropolitan Chicago.

language on financing after they had thoroughly considered the subject.

Few specific wordings were submitted either by mail from these experts or from others speaking on finance. The Welfare Council of Metropolitan Chicago gave its support to the wording of Member Proposal 434. Prof. G. Alan Hickrod of Illinois State University asked that the constitution remain silent on the subject, stating that this was an area for legislative determination which should not be resolved by the courts. The Illinois Association of School Administrators suggested this wording:

> The Legislature shall provide only for the support and maintenance of a system of free public schools guaranteeing equal educational opportunity and open to all children in the State.

Research indicated that of the twenty-three state constitutions which mentioned school revenue, almost all referred in general terms to the funds which should be used to support the public schools or directed the legislature to make suitable provision for financing education. The only more precise references were in the Oklahoma and California constitutions, which specifically stated the per capita amount to be supplied by the state for each student or the lowest per capita amount to be allowed.

Despite these findings, the Committee on Education was obviously moved by the statistics discussed above and by statements of witnesses describing the plight of the schools to try to alleviate some of these financial problems. Urban delegates on the committee had long recognized the plight of inner city schools. Eloquent testimony from witnesses helped to awaken others to the situation. The main point, however, was that almost all schools, not just those in the cities, were in need of greater financial assistance. The issue of financing of the public schools had not been discussed during the early committee meetings. Yet, as discussion proceeded, it was obvious that all members felt a genuine concern over this issue.

SUPERFICIAL CONSENSUS TURNS TO DISCORD

That the committee would again become divided into factions was not obvious at the inception of the discussion. Bottino was the first to insist that financing receive careful scrutiny. As early as March

13 he commented on the neglect of the subject and as chairman of the subcommittee on financing it was he who requested most of the research that was done. Early discussions indicated that all committee members were disturbed about the issue but that, because of its complexity, no one knew how to handle it constitutionally.

On June 2 a hand vote was taken on this language, submitted by Fogal:

> To meet the goals in Section One the State shall provide the total financial support of public education through the secondary level.

Six members voted in favor of the language (Fogal, Dove, Howard, Parker, Patch, and Pughsley), two were opposed (Buford and Evans), and one voted present (Kamin). Mathias and Bottino were absent. At this point Fogal and Patch were the most insistent upon total state financing of education, and Fogal stated on the author's questionnaire that he had no position on this issue prior to the convention and that his stand was almost entirely influenced by Patch.

The ensuing change of positions is somewhat difficult to analyze. Although Bottino had orginally been vociferously in favor of a great degree of change in the system of financing of the public schools (as he indicated in May in reply to the author's questionnaire), in June he joined Evans, Buford, and Mathias in opposing total state financing. On June 2, Parker voted for Fogal's wording, which called for full support of education from the state level; but he too later joined the other members of the Old Guard in opposing the concept of total funding provided by the state.

Delegate Dove had originally voted for Fogal's wording, but he indicated later to the author that he had not been in favor of the proposal. Also, in response to the author's questionnaire, which he returned in August, he stated:

> Although I was responsible for bringing the "full state financing" issue to a head, I don't really approve of it at least as of today. I believe it will gradually come in the future. I was a little disturbed when it was changed to ninety per cent to increase its "salability." I was a little afraid that it might pass — but my intuition correctly informed me it would not. I was amused by the stir that it caused.

Kamin was also basically of the opinion that financing was a legislative matter. Kamin was a product of the Evanston, Illinois, school system, one which is reputed to be among the finest in the country. He privately voiced apprehension about what total state financing might do to such a school system, fearing that it might bring all school systems to a level of mediocrity rather than raise the poor ones to a higher level. Nevertheless, Kamin and Dove spoke in favor of the position adopted by the Young Turks. Therefore, only Fogal, Patch, and Howard, of the younger members, were originally totally committed to full state financing of the public schools.

These positions resulted from political gamesmanship on the part of both groups. Bottino and Parker joined the other members of the Old Guard in opposing total state financing. Their reasons for doing so may have been more a result of the distrust they felt for the Young Turks and the fact that they did not want to vote with these younger members than of their opposition to the concept of total state financing.[7] There is evidence of this possibility in the fact that Parker and Bottino offered amendments at the full convention very similar to the Young Turks' final suggestion of 90 percent state support.

Among the younger group, political gamesmanship was most particularly exhibited by Dove, whose remark about his amusement over the "stir" that total state financing caused has been referred to. This remark and others which he made privately show that he was not totally committed to the concept of full state financing. Kamin eventually joined the other members of the Young Turks in their support of the concept, but did not commit himself until a ruling was announced on the floor of the convention that all committee reports had to be in by the following week. Reputedly this announcement was made at the instigation of Mathias, and the younger members felt that in so doing he was trying to prevent them from presenting any proposal on financing. Irritated at this development, Kamin then joined the other Young Turks, since he considered it necessary that the full convention give some attention to financing of the public schools. His original hesitation had been due

---

[7] In addition, it was rumored Bottino's enthusiasm for total state support waned after a conference with Governor Ogilvie, who opposed the concept.

to a feeling that the proposal was basically legislative in nature.[8] This gave the younger group the majority position, for Pughsley had returned and was voting with the Young Turks on this issue.

These were the reasons given by those opting for total state support of education: First, such a system would tend to equalize tax ratios in the state. Second, it would permit redrawing of school district boundaries into more efficient units, without so great a concern for tax consequences. Third, it would permit all districts to benefit from the taxes paid by industry. Fourth, the burden of tax free property in districts would be equalized. Fifth, it would permit local school boards and administrators to concentrate their efforts on educational matters rather than on the yearly fights for budgets and bond issues. Sixth, it would produce a level of educational opportunity that would be more equal throughout the state for all children. It was the sixth point with which the delegates were mainly concerned. The rest was just "icing on the cake" as one member put it.

Pressure and Gamesmanship Generate Resolution

The press, in various newspaper articles, reported the proposal of the Young Turks, and public disapproval began to be voiced. Delegates were confronted by their constituents when they returned home over the weekend, and letters and telegrams expressing opposition to full state financing were sent to the committee. In the face of public reaction, most of which was stated in the form of outrage over the fear of loss of local control from such a proposal, the members of the younger group changed from a position of total state financing to one in which 90 percent of the financing would come from the state:

> To meet the goals of Section One, substantially all funds for the operational costs of the free public schools shall be appropriated by the General Assembly for the benefit of the local school districts. No local governmental unit or school district may levy taxes or appropriate funds for the purposes of such educational operation except to the extent of ten per cent (10%) of the

[8] Malcolm Kamin, in interviews with the author, July–August 1970.

amount received by that district from the General Assembly in that year.

However, even with this change, Evans, Mathias, Buford, Parker and Bottino still refused to join the majority (Kamin, Dove, Patch, Fogal, Howard, and Pughsley). Their reasons were first, that such a provision is a legislative matter; second, that the General Assembly had already been continually increasing funds for schools, and the majority plan would only endanger the tradition of local control of public schools; third, the majority position would result in a leveling and a standardization of the educational programs of the public schools; fourth, that it would cause decreased local interest in schools; fifth, that this proposal would require greatly increased taxes or the implementation of new taxes; sixth, that such a plan is virtually untried and should not be frozen into the constitution. Despite these objections the majority report calling for 90 percent financing from the state was presented to the full convention. The minority — the Old Guard — wrote a report asking for the defeat of the proposal of the Young Turks.

On this issue can again be seen the conflict over the degree of change which was to be incorporated into the education article. Delegates Buford, Evans, and Mathias were against anything so radical as total state financing, and they convinced Parker and Bottino to join their ranks. That these two delegates were so persuaded gives some support to the claim of political gamesmanship among these members; they did not want to be a part of the opposite "team." Delegates Kamin and Dove, of the younger members, were not totally committed to the concept of full state financing due to their feelings that it was basically a legislative matter and to their apprehension as to the results it might cause. Dove exhibited political gamesmanship in his support of the concept, as has been shown by his questionnaire response. He, like Bottino and Parker, did not want to join the opposing "team." Friendship with the other Young Turks would have made it difficult for him to do so, even had he wanted to. Delegate Kamin eventually joined the other younger members — partially, perhaps, out of feelings of camaraderie, but also because he felt that the full convention should give its attention to the issue of financing of the public schools. That this was also a part of Dove's motivation is shown by another response from his questionnaire:

> Although properly a legislative matter I believe the Committee acted in a responsible manner in its proposal. This is one of the many areas which the legislature cannot research fully and full state financing of education will most likely never be reached without constitutional mandate.

The result of the split into factions was ultimately beneficial, for it meant that the finance section reported to the floor of the convention was one which provided a radical starting point for discussion. If the committee had reached a less innovative position through compromise, it is possible the convention might have included no mention of financing in the final education article. In interviews with the author at the outset of the convention, most delegates had indicated that they saw financing as a legislative matter. Yet, as will be shown in the next chapter, the full convention was forced to consider the issue. The delegates were shown the disgraceful plight of many schools in Illinois. Support for the concept of total state financing grew, and although the resulting section on finance in the education article may be considered hortatory in nature, it at least shows the concern which materialized during the convention.[9]

[9] For a summary of court interpretation of these financing provisions, see the discussion of the legal battle over school financing in Chapter IX, *infra*.

VII

The Education Article at First Reading

As reported from committee on April 14 the education article read:

Section 1. Goal — Free Schools

The paramount goal of the people of the State shall be the educational development of all persons to the limits of their capacities.

To achieve this goal, it shall be the duty of the State to provide for an efficient system of high quality public educational institutions and services.

Education in the public schools through the secondary level shall be free. There may be such other free education as the General Assembly provides.

Section 2. State Board of Education — Chief State Educational Officer

There shall be a State Board of Education selected on a regional basis. The number of members, their qualifications, terms of office and manner of selection shall be provided by law. The Board shall establish goals, determine policies, provide for planning and evaluating educational programs, recommend financing and have such jurisdiction, powers, and duties as provided by law.

There shall be a chief state educational officer appointed by the State Board of Education.

Section 3. Public Funds for Sectarian Purposes Forbidden

Neither the General Assembly nor any county, city, town, township, school district, or other public corporation, shall ever make any appropriation or pay from any public fund whatever, anything in aid of any church or sectarian purpose, or to help support or sustain any school, academy, seminary, college, university, or other literary or scientific institution, controlled by any church or sectarian denomination whatever; nor shall any grant or donation of land, money, or other personal property ever be made by the State, or any such public corporation, to any church, or for any sectarian purpose.

In addition to these sections, which were considered as Proposal 1, the younger members of the committee reported Proposal 2, containing the following section, to the floor of the convention on July 22:

Section 4.

To meet the goals of Section 1, substantially all funds for the operational costs of the free public schools shall be appropriated by the General Assembly for the benefit of the local school districts. No local governmental unit or school district may levy taxes or appropriate funds for the purposes of such educational operation except to the extent of ten per cent (10%) of the amount received by that district from the General Assembly in that year.

SECTION 1, EDUCATIONAL OBJECTIVES

The Education Committee followed the standard procedure of assigning the presentation and explanation of each section to the convention to certain of its members. Section 1 was presented to the convention on April 22 by Patch and Fogal — the two members of the committee who had originally been the most interested in producing a strong statement of goals. Both delegates gave a thorough explanation of the section, stressing the need for education, the rights of the underprivileged, and the fact that the state had not been fulfilling its responsibilities in this area.

Fogal emphasized that the third paragraph of section 1 meant all people — not just children as in the 1870 document — were to be entitled to free education through the secondary level. In addition, he stressed that the third paragraph provided for changing conditions by allowing the General Assembly to make other forms or levels of education free when needed.[1]

There were fifteen questions directed to the committee in regard to section 1. Many were of a miscellaneous nature, such as whether using the term "efficient" would incorporate the law which had grown up around this word in the 1870 constitution. The committee felt it would. Many questions — and those most significant for the following debate — dealt with the word "paramount" and with whether the section was a mandate to the General Assembly to provide for the educational development of all persons. One delegate asked whether the first paragraph of section 1 was in the nature of a preamble which should be included in the preamble to the whole document. To the committee, "paramount" meant education would be the number one goal of the state, funded before all other programs. They insisted the first paragraph was meant to be an operative mandate to the General Assembly, not simply a preamble.

In regard to the word "free," the convention was most concerned to know if the word referred to anything other than tuition in the elementary and secondary schools. Fogal responded:

> You may recall earlier in our committee deliberations we voted tentatively to strike "free," since most of us recognize that we don't have — and as far as I know we have never had — totally free public schools; and we reconsidered that earlier position. We felt that tradition will continue, probably, to interpret "free public education" as we always have, and it's open to either provide totally free education, whether you are speaking of book fees, book rentals, or PE equipment, or we can continue as we are now, I don't think we have changed it.

During the debates on section 1 on April 23, six amendments were offered; all of them sought to remove or to modify "para-

---

[1] References to the debates and proceedings of the Sixth Illinois Constitutional Convention have not been specifically noted in this or the following chapters. The reader who wishes to read through the debates on the education article will find most of the formative process described herein in the verbatim transcripts for April 22–24 and 28, May 6, and August 4, 13, and 31. See Sixth Illinois Constitutional Convention, *Record of Proceedings*, 1970, Vol. II, pp. 749–837, 839–862, and 923–949; Vol. IV, pp. 3535–3586; and Vol. V, pp. 4105–4182 and 4457–4528.

mount." An amendment to paragraphs one and two of the committee report was suggested by Stanley Johnson, a Republican from DeKalb:

> The State shall provide for an efficient system of high-quality educational institutions and services.

In defending this amendment Johnson explained that, although he was in total agreement with all Patch had said about the importance of education, it seemed to him that "the paramount goal is to create a society of which education is just one part." Johnson's amendment also removed the word "public" from the second paragraph, so the state could resort to other than public institutions in order to educate its citizens if necessary. With no other delegates speaking in favor of his amendment, and after an eloquent defense of the committee's section by Patch, Johnson felt forced to say, "I knew that I was going to uncover a hornet's nest when I offered this, and Delegate Patch's once-again display of eloquence puts us all who might want to vote for this amendment in the very peculiar position of voting against good education for everyone." The amendment was defeated by a voice vote.

The second amendment, offered by David Davis, a Republican from Bloomington, left the second and third paragraphs of section 1 of the committee proposal intact, but substituted for the first paragraph:

> The educational development of all persons to the limits of their capacities is a matter of major concern and importance to the State of Illinois and the residents thereof.

The debate again centered on the fact that other activities of the state could also be considered paramount. Although receiving more support from other delegates than did the previous amendment, the suggestion failed by a hand count of fifty-six to forty-three.

The third amendment, submitted by Mary Pappas, a Republican from Lake Bluff, proposed to change "the paramount" to "a paramount." The amendment received some support, but was called "nit picking" and grammatically incorrect, in that paramount suggests the highest with no others equal to it. The amendment was defeated by a voice vote.

The fourth amendment, a culmination of many suggestions made during the debate, was offered by George Lewis, a Democrat from Quincy. Lewis proposed changing "the paramount" to "a fundamental." He declared: "We should not leave a word that does not really connote what we do believe about a free society, and that is we believe that life, liberty, and happiness are *the* paramount goal, and education is a means to that goal." Having received almost no opposition from committee members and with the support of all other delegates who spoke on it, this amendment passed seventy-four to twenty-seven on a hand vote.

Another amendment, by Clifford Downen, would have deleted the entire committee proposal and substituted the wording of section 1 of the 1870 constitution; it was defeated seventy-nine to twelve. Also rejected, but by a voice vote, was an amendment by Michael Madigan which stated:

A fundamental goal of the People of the State shall be the educational development of all persons to the limits of their capacities, whether this educational development be academic, vocational, technical or otherwise.

Lewis's insertion of "a fundamental" in place of "the paramount" was a major change from the intention of the committee proposal. Many committee members were not upset but relieved when the change was made, whereas others were thankful that nothing else had been altered.[2] Only Delegate Patch seemed greatly disappointed.

Few of the delegates at the full convention wished to be branded as voting "against education," as is shown by the responses of those who were interviewed. Many of them felt that the language of section 1 was too idealistic, that in addition to the word "paramount," the goal of educating people "to the limits of their capacities" was immeasurable and fruitless. However, they were content to make only a change of two words, leaving the rest of the section as reported from committee. In providing an education article which was, at least, strongly worded, they were showing their constituents that they were "for education." As one delegate told the author in

[2] Mathias was rumored to be working against section 1 because of its strong language.

confidence: "If I had voted against this section, there would have been hell to pay at home — and not just from the educators. Education at the moment is just too hot to handle. I almost felt forced to vote for "paramount." Whether the wording is or is not overly idealistic may be determined if and when Illinois courts hear suits brought under the section. It will be of interest to discover what interpretation is given to the words "fundamental" and "to the limits of their capacities."

After first reading, therefore, section 1 read:

> A fundamental goal of the People of the State shall be the educational development of all persons to the limits of their capacities.
>
> To achieve this goal, it shall be the duty of the State to provide for an efficient system of high quality public educational institutions and services.
>
> Education in the public schools through the secondary level shall be free. There may be such other free education as the General Assembly provides.

SECTION 2, STATE BOARD OF EDUCATION

Section 2 was presented to the convention by Buford and Evans on April 20. Buford emphasized that various aspects — such as manner of selection, powers, duties, and jurisdiction of the board — had been left to the General Assembly because the committee couldn't reach agreement and felt the full convention would also be divided. He pointed out that only the Illinois Federation of Teachers was opposed to the creation of such a board. Evans spoke of the necessity for a truly professional chief state school officer and of the fact that a state board would take over many duties from the overburdened office of superintendent of public instruction.

There were fifteen questions directed to the committee concerning section 2. Most dealt with the selection and jurisdiction of the board, showing that, as in committee, these areas of section 2 seemed to be the most controversial. The committee members reiterated that since neither method of selection was demonstrably superior, the determination should be left to the General Assembly. In regard to jurisdiction the committee emphasized that no power was being taken away from local boards of education, and that whether the board's authority should extend to the university level or only to elementary and secondary education should not be frozen into the constitution. The committee was asked whether there was really a need for such a board, to which Kamin replied:

> In our first section, the statement is that "education is the paramount duty of the state." ... it is the state's primary obligation and duty to look after education, and therefore a *state* agency which is devoted *fully* to education is the best means of expressing this. ... The movement is for more ... centralization of education at the state level, and this is what we feel the board would provide.

During the debate on section 2 on April 24 there were seven amendments offered. By far the most lengthy and significant debate was over appointment versus election of the chief educational officer, as well as of the board members themselves. The particular amendment which provoked the most discussion was suggested by Robert Butler, a Republican from Marion:

> There shall be a State Board of Education elected from districts. The number of members, their qualifications, terms of office, and manner of election shall be determined by law.

Originally the proposal had stated "by non-partisan ballot" and "on a regional basis," but Butler had accepted changes from the floor.

The arguments for and against the amendment were generally the same as the arguments in committee over appointment versus election. In defense of his proposal Butler declared:

> I propose this amendment because I believe in the principle that when the taxpayers' dollars are spent, the taxpayers should be guaranteed a direct voice in the manner in which their money is spent. ... I do not believe we were elected delegates to this Convention for the purpose of passing on to another body the matter of making decisions. ... Why not let the people who foot the bill be guaranteed by their constitution that the persons who set the policy for education in Illinois will be directly responsible to the will of the people of Illinois? After all, if there is one fundamental truth upon which we can all agree, it is that they who

must face the voters at the ballot box at regular intervals will most quickly heed the voice of the people between elections.

Speaking against the Butler amendment, David Kenney, a Republican from Carbondale, stated:

> The decision we are asked to make here is not one between election and appointment ... but the choice is one between specifying election of this board and permitting the General Assembly to specify the method of choice — either election or appointment. ...
> In short, I believe that the committee's proposal gives the elected General Assembly ... the maximum freedom to design a state board of education which will serve us best, and I am always suspicious of those who would freeze a particular form into the constitution. I sometimes have the feeling that in so doing they seek a personal advantage and may perhaps be wishing to deny the public, through its elected representatives, the maximum freedom in seeking the best arrangement.

In support of the committee proposal Dove added that it would be a mistake to provide for the election of the board without knowing its exact powers and duties. Kamin suggested that an elected board, stipulated in the constitution, would foreclose the possibility of having the governor, the superintendent of schools or former superintendents, or other educational and legislative officers serve as ex officio members — a system which had proved helpful in other states.

Only a sampling of the discussion of this amendment has been provided; the debate occupies almost a hundred pages in the transcript. However, the general and most important arguments have been given: guaranteeing power and representation to the people versus providing for flexibility and change at a future date. The divisive nature of the question is apparent from the closeness of the vote — fifty-two members voted in favor of the Butler amendment, fifty-four against.

Since a roll call vote was requested on the issue, it is possible to analyze the vote in order to determine some reasons for the narrow defeat of the amendment. Deletion of any mention of nonpartisan ballot had been proposed by David Stahl, a member of the Chicago Democratic organization, which often opposes nonpartisan elections. (They had, for instance, opposed a nonpartisan constitutional convention.) It is logical that any organization which controlled an area as decisively as the Democrats controlled Chicago in 1970 would favor partisan elections to be sure its chosen representatives were selected. In Illinois, as was evidenced by those delegates who spoke on other issues which dealt with election versus appointment of officials, two other groups usually favor election — blacks and downstaters. On this amendment, however, the traditional pattern did not develop. Whereas most Chicago Democrats voted in favor of the proposal, six were opposed. Most blacks (including Patch) voted for it, but five voted against. Again, most downstaters were in favor of the Butler proposal, but there were many exceptions.

There are two likely explanations for this vote. First, the delegates were not really voting for election and against appointment, but rather for election and against letting the legislature determine the issue. It is conceivable that the appeal of flexibility was great enough to overcome any strong stance on election or appointment. As Davis explained:

> Let me say that originally I had planned to offer an amendment here to provide for an appointive board and to take away from the legislature the right to determine the method of selection. I am persuaded by what has been said here this morning that it is essential that we leave this ultimate decision to the legislature, not only in the first instance, but for the purpose of change in the event that the legislature finds at some future date that change is dictated by the circumstances which may later arise.

Secondly, the special nature of the subject of education may have overcome the traditional biases on election and appointment. Many delegates who might otherwise have favored election alluded to the need for educational experts and for special consideration in the area of education, which might not be provided through the elective process.[3] In this, as in other respects, education was considered "different," in that standards distinct from those used for other issues were to be employed.

Much argument took place on an amendment offered by Wen-

---

[3] Buford, a strong proponent of the elective method, made an exception for education, as did James Thompson, Charles Coleman, and Paul Elward. Interviews with the author, April 1970.

dell Durr, a Democrat from Edwardsville, which would have substituted the following for the committee proposal:

> There shall be a full-time State Board of Education elected on a regional basis. The number of members, their qualifications, compensation and terms of office shall be determined by law.
>
> The members of the Board shall be elected at general elections. The Board shall establish goals, determine policies, provide for planning and evaluating educational programs, recommend financing and have such jurisdiction, powers and duties as provided by law.
>
> The Board shall choose one of its members as a chief state educational officer, on such basis, with such powers, and for such term as the Board determines.

The amendment originally stated "elected by non-partisan ballot," but again the deletion was suggested by one of the Chicago Democrats and was agreed to.

Durr asserted that his amendment was meant to do three things: ensure that the people themselves would control the education of their children; require a board which would devote full time to its task; and provide for an education officer who would be responsive to the people. Kamin responded that requiring a full time board would in fact be creating a fourth branch of government, and that requiring the chief education officer to come from among the members could destroy the whole concept of a professional officer to lead education in the state. The amendment was defeated by a roll call vote of sixty-eight to thirty-four.

This vote was not a reliable indicator of delegate positions, however, because it included more than one change from the committee report. One delegate who had previously voted against the Butler proposal voted yes on this amendment, but fifteen who had earlier voted yes were against the Durr suggestion. Of those against, nine were Chicago Democrats; neither Durr's amendment nor the Butler proposal was apparently a "party" issue. Nor was there bloc voting along racial, religious, sex, age, or occupational lines on the Durr or Butler amendments. The lack of any strict division along these lines again would seem to indicate that education was thought to be "different."

The only amendment to section 2 of the committee proposal

which succeeded was offered by Helen Kinney, a Republican from Hinsdale who often voted with the Democrats. The Kinney amendment added "elected or" before the word "selected" in the committee proposal, thus making the wording "there shall be a State Board of Education elected or selected on a regional basis." Although the committee insisted that "selected" was a neutral word intended to refer to both appointment and election, Kinney felt the addition was needed to make section 2 correspond to the wording of the judicial article. The amendment passed by a hand vote of forty-eight to thirty-four. Although the amendment was purportedly just for means of clarification, it should be noted that Kinney was consistently on the side of those favoring the elective method, and thus her intention may have been to make it more likely or easier for the General Assembly to choose election.

The final version of section 2 after first reading was

There shall be a State Board of Education elected or selected on a regional basis. The number of members, their qualifications, terms of office and manner of selection shall be provided by law. The Board shall establish goals, determine policies, provide for planning and evaluating educational programs, recommend financing and have such jurisdiction, powers and duties as provided by law.

There shall be a chief state educational officer appointed by the State Board of Education.

SECTION 3, AID TO NONPUBLIC SCHOOLS

The explanation of section 3 on aid to nonpublic schools was presented for the committee by Kamin and Howard. Howard summarized the report on the section, listing the approaches considered in committee. As discussed earlier in this manuscript, the committee had rejected making the section more restrictive for fear of invalidating certain existing programs. Yet the courts in some cases had already shown themselves hesitant to uphold any language less restrictive than the federal First Amendment, so committee members felt liberalizing the section would have raised the political controversy incident to change without effecting any actual change in the legal status of aid to nonpublic schools. Since the existing section had been interpreted as no more restrictive than the First Amendment, the committee chose the alternative of leaving that section unchanged. That decision, they thought, would reaffirm the traditional separation of church and state while allowing any programs that are constitutional under the First Amendment. Howard also pointed out that major organizations on both sides of this issue had asked that the section remain unchanged.

There were twenty-nine questions addressed to the committee on section 3. Most of them were attempts to ascertain exactly what the committee report meant, for the language of section 3, especially to nonlawyers, appeared much more prohibitive than the committee claimed. Kamin explained that although the language was restrictive, the Illinois courts had previously interpreted certain programs of support as permissible in that they aided the child rather than the institution. He emphasized that each particular program in the future would have to be considered separately to see if it met this criterion.

Kamin also made these interpretations in the course of the discussion: first, in the opinion of the committee, the Illinois Supreme Court would follow the lead of the United States Supreme Court in deciding how much aid could be allowed; the words "support" or "aid" in the Illinois Constitution would be interpreted in the same way that the word "establish" in the federal First Amendment is understood. Second, although a change in the wording, such as the substitution of the First Amendment, might make the section more clear, any change in such an emotional issue — even one that was not substantial — might be to the detriment of the ratification of the constitution as a whole. In addition, because the decision ultimately rested with the United States Supreme Court, "the retention or deletion of this language is not . . . determinative in any way of the question of what programs of aid are constitutional and what programs of aid are not constitutional." Third, although it is possible that the Illinois Supreme Court could interpret the language of section 3 as being very restrictive, and although the United States Supreme Court could in the future place a more restrictive interpretation on the meaning of the word "establish," it was the assumption of the committee that the courts would continue to follow the precedents they had established in this field.

Republican Thomas Miller from South Holland asked:

> Of the organizations who testified before your committee, were
> there any who favored retention of the present language because
> they feel that public aid in some direct or indirect form to the
> private school system is constitutionally possible?

In answer Kamin stated:

> I would have to say that — yes, most of them, to the extent that
> we spoke categorically with them — to the extent that we asked,
> as we did ask, virtually every witness who testified before us, "Do
> you understand that under this language we now have school
> bussing [sic] in Illinois for parochial schools?" And they said,
> "Yes, we understand that." We said, "Do you understand that
> there are school lunch programs? Do you understand that there
> is a state scholarship program existing under this language?"
> They said yes they did, and they understood.

Kamin seemed to be implying that all of those who testified on this
question were fully cognizant of forms of aid being extended at
that time under section 3. Although presumably most educational
experts and organizations testifying against aid were aware of previous court interpretations and of the fact that the language might
not be interpreted as strictly as it would appear, it is doubtful if
the ordinary citizen who testified against aid or the citizens who
would be voting on the new constitution were so cognizant. Even
though the committee had attempted to make all witnesses aware
of existing aid, it is especially likely that the laymen did not realize
court interpretations had left open the possibility of more extensive
aid, such as the voucher or the payment of services plans. Yet even
the experts and organizations — those against aid as well as those
in favor — were willing to permit the section to remain unchanged,
thus leaving final determination to the courts.

In response to a statement from Arthur Lennon, a Catholic Republican from Joliet, that the issue was really a legislative matter,
Kamin agreed that this might be one reason for deleting section 3;
but he defended the committee's recommendation by pointing to
the difficulty of explaining that consideration to nonexperts. In
answer to a delegate who suggested that separate submission must
be the solution to the dilemma, Kamin declared:

What we feel is that any attempt to submit this question as a separate question . . . is going to, in fact, place a false issue before the people; because . . . the retention or deletion of this language is not, as we have indicated, determinative in any way of the question of what programs of aid are constitutional and what programs of aid are not constitutional.

Though leaving the section unchanged involved some of the same misrepresentation, Kamin thought the costs of changing the wording might have proved greater than the costs of slightly misleading the citizenry. As the section stood, both sides felt their aims were being accomplished. The citizens could direct their outrage at future court interpretations rather than at the proposed constitution.

There were only three amendments offered when the committee proposal on section 3 was perfected April 28. Michael Madigan, a Catholic Chicago Democrat, suggested:

The State shall make no law respecting an establishment of religion, or prohibiting the free exercise thereof.

The amendment was ruled out of order because it did not refer to education.

Lennon then proposed to delete section 3 from the constitution. Surprisingly the debates on the deletion of the section were of a mild, unemotional nature. The one exception was a lengthy diatribe by Father Francis Lawlor, a Catholic priest from Chicago's southwest side, who pointed out the benefits provided by nonpublic schools and the "double taxation" paid by those who send their children to them. The main points raised by those supporting deletion were that the section was legislative in nature, and that it presented the issue in a restrictive manner which was perhaps deceiving. As Lennon stated in defense of his amendment:

I have talked to Mr. Kamin and other members of the Education Committee. I have studied and looked at their report, and I think it is a good report. . . . They say, in effect, "don't rock the boat." And that is a good, practical, political reason not to do something. . . . The fact remains, though, from a purely and simply constitutional view point . . . that this type of provision in a constitution is nothing less or more than unenforceable legislation and probably the result of medieval bigotry, no more and no less. . . .

So I suggest that, really, what we have gotten to is a rationalization of doing what we want to do, contrary to the obvious intention of the language of our present constitution.

Kamin replied that the question of whether or not to delete the language is really a posing of the question on separation of church and state, which is unarguable since it is provided for by the federal Constitution. To suggest deletion would, he said, raise a false issue, since the federal language is the ultimate determining criterion.

While the majority of the members were opposed to deletion, some delegates voted for retention of the wording of the section for reasons other than those presented in the committee report. Bernard Weisberg, a Jew who — as a Chicago attorney — was cognizant of court decisions and legal ramifications, stated:

> I would like to state my disagreement with the committee report's interpretation of article VIII, section 3. I do not believe that this Convention has authority to make any statement about the intention of the present constitutional provision which will be entitled to any weight in the courts. If, however, the courts do, some day, look to our debates, they should note that many of the delegates who vote today to retain article VIII, section 3, do so because we believe it means what it says, and because we believe that it expresses wise policy.

Clyde Parker of the Education Committee seemed to be in agreement with Weisberg, rather than with the committee report. He declared, "The language is clear. And it can be understood. And if it is a part of the basic law of our state, then I, for one, believe it should be followed and that devious ways to get around it should not be created."

The amendment to delete the section failed by a roll call vote of seventy-nine to thirty-five. The vote was not strictly along party lines, although the majority of white Chicago Democrats voted for it, nor was it solidly along Catholic versus non-Catholic lines, since some Catholics voted against deletion, quite possibly out of fear that increased aid to nonpublic schools would increase segregation.[4]

Other reasons for the vote, as given by the delegates interviewed, were diverse: the majority of those questioned who voted against

[4] Samuel Patch, in an interview with the author.

deletion agreed with the committee that controversy should be avoided since deletion would not make a substantive difference; others, such as Weisberg, Parker, Friedrich, and Garrison, intended their votes as an affirmation of their support of the existing language at its face value. Of those voting for deletion who were questioned, some members, such as Lennon, Thompson, and Young, felt that aid to nonpublic schools was a legislative matter; but the majority of those interviewed who favored deletion did so because they hoped more aid to nonpublic schools would be possible without the 1870 wording. Those so indicating were Arrigo, Daley, Elward, Gierach, Knuppel, Laurino, Lyons, Madigan, Miska, Strunk, Tuchow, and Tomei. Tomei, a Catholic, was the only member of the Independent bloc who voted in favor of deletion. The other delegates mentioned with Tomei were all Democrats, and all but Tuchow were Catholics.

Debate over the only other amendment was short. That proposal, offered by Helen Kinney, would have added this qualification after the words "shall ever" and "purpose" in the committee proposal:

> ... in any manner which conflicts with the provision in the Constitution of the United States prohibiting the making of any law respecting the establishment of religion.

This amendment failed without further debate by a hand vote of fifty-nine to twenty-six.

In general the debates show that, by contrast with 1870, there was little overt religious prejudice at work. Rather, the delegates themselves seem to have been motivated by other factors, such as the economic situation, constitutional purity, and the desire to placate the voters. However, in their wish to avoid controversy and to please the voters, they may have been giving in to their constituents, some of whom were motivated by religious prejudice or by misinformation (as had been demonstrated by such organizations as Americans United for Separation of Church and State). However, the retention of language written in an era of high religious feeling was not in itself a sign of religious prejudice, since the delegates knew final interpretation would be left to the courts. It does indicate that the delegates were willing to retain confusing wording written in a more bigoted era in order to please the voters and to ensure that controversy would not endanger the ratification of the constitution. Here, as with most other educational issues discussed by the full convention, the main basis for decision was apparently the perceived will of the voters and the necessity felt by the delegates to placate them.

DELETIONS FROM THE 1870 ARTICLE

The deletion of sections 2, 4, and 5 of the education article of the 1870 constitution caused little discussion at the full convention, although some delegates would have preferred to see section 2 retained. This section read:

> All lands, moneys, or other property, donated, granted or received for school, college, seminary or university purposes, and the proceeds thereof, shall be faithfully applied to the objects for which such gifts or grants were made.

In explaining the committee's proposal to delete section 2, Dove pointed out the very limited application of the section and said the committee considered it an area of intergovernmental taxation and more properly a legislative matter. The questions raised on this section were few, but it was noted that some townships had gone to particular trouble to preserve lands under this provision so the income arising from the property could be applied to the reduction of school taxes levied against the owners of property within that township.

The points raised about this section were sufficient to cause the committee, on April 28, to ask for a postponement of debate on the section until the matter could be considered more thoroughly. Between April 28 and May 6 the committee reexamined its recommendation to delete section 2 and heard testimony from experts, in particular from Delegate Thomas McCracken, a Cook County deputy assessor. All testifying experts supported the committee proposal to remove the section.

Debate was heard on the section again on May 6, at which time the committee reiterated its recommendation to delete. Some members of the committee suggested adding a provision in the schedule — that part of the constitution which stipulated when various provisions were to take effect — that the section should continue to be active for those counties with land applicable under this part of the charter:

> The provision of section 2 of article VIII of the Constitution of Illinois effective August 8, 1870, shall continue in force and effect as to all lands, monies, or other property donated, granted or received from school, college, seminary or university purposes prior to August 8, 1870, and the proceeds thereof.

This was not a unanimous position of the committee, however, and a minority (Dove, Fogal, and Howard) wished for no mention of this subject in the schedule.

The vote on the motion to delete section 2 was carried eighty-four to two, with no discussion. Debate was heard, however, on the scheduling proposal. Speaking for the minority of the committee which did not favor this provision, Dove pointed out that since any lands used for school purposes are exempt from taxation under the revenue article, only those lands acquired for school purposes prior to 1870 which were now used for nonschool purposes would be affected. The total income from these lands in 1969 amounted to $1,330,000. Dove explained that if this section were removed and the property became taxable, most of the tax money would be returned to the schools, in any case, since the schools were the major recipient of such tax money. Secondly, he pointed out that although these lands were exempt from special and benefit taxation as well as general assessment, in 1969 the legislature had passed a law which provided that the lessee or occupant of any real property which is privately used and for any reason exempt from taxation must pay a "use tax" equivalent to the amount of a real property tax. The use tax thus in large part negated the special effects of section 2. Dove also emphasized that a constitution is for the whole state and not for the particular protection of one group or another.

The main argument in favor of the provision in the schedule was supplied by David Davis, who had a special interest in West Township, McLean County, which had preserved its 640 acres of section 16 land, plus 80 acres added after the original grant, intact. Davis explained it was likely the legislature would direct that these lands be sold and the proceeds distributed not to the townships which had preserved the lands but to the entire school district. The view of the minority of the committee prevailed, however, and the motion to include a provision dealing with section 2 in the schedule was defeated by a hand vote of sixty-six to twenty-five.

Section 4 of the 1870 constitution was deleted on April 28 by a vote of eighty-nine to zero and section 5 was deleted the same day by the vote of eighty-one to zero.

PROPOSAL 2: SCHOOL FINANCING

The only other educational matter to be debated at first reading was Proposal 2, on school financing, suggested by Fogal, Patch, Howard, Dove, Kamin, and Pughsley:

> Section 4.
>
> To meet the goals of Section 1, substantially all funds for the operational costs of the free public schools shall be appropriated by the General Assembly for the benefit of the local school districts. No local governmental unit or school district may levy taxes or appropriate funds for the purposes of such educational operation except to the extent of ten percent (10%) of the amount received by that district from the General Assembly in that year.

Mathias, Evans, Bottino, Buford, and Parker proposed a minority report that asked for the deletion of the above wording.

This subject was presented to the full convention as a second report because it came so much later than the other sections on education (August instead of April or May). It was the last matter to be considered by the convention at first reading. Tempers were short and frustration was high among the delegates, who had expected to finish all of their business by August 8, when most of the money for the convention would give out. On August 4, however, they had not yet even completed first reading.

Discussion on the topic of financing of public schools was lengthy; it occupies three hundred thirty-two pages of the transcript of August 4. The presentation for the majority of the committee was made by Kamin, Howard, Dove, and Fogal. Kamin stressed that this was a well thought out proposal, not — as he said various newspapers had been charging — some "last-minute idea that some long haired idealist dreamed up." He pointed out that the proposal was meant to accomplish two things — reduction of the burden of the real and personal property taxes on the farmer and the homeowner and equalization of educational opportunities throughout the state. Rather than being of a legislative nature, the proposal had constitutional significance because "it is unlikely that the General Assembly would ever adopt a plan which focuses political pressure on it for more money when it could continue with a plan where political pressure is divided between itself and the local communities."

Howard addressed herself to the financial crisis of the Illinois schools, saying, "No student in the State of Illinois should be denied an adequate educational opportunity because of the accident of local tax property geography." Dove described how the proposal would work, predicting that the effect of the committee proposal would be to reduce local taxes which had been levied for educational purposes by approximately 68 percent. He explained that in 1969 Illinois ranked forty-third out of the fifty states in the amount of revenue supplied by the state for educational purposes. The national average was well over 40 percent, whereas the state in Illinois contributed only 25 percent.

Fogal spoke on the impact the committee proposal would have on local control: "Local control, the committee supports wholeheartedly. We have no desire and no intention in changing this traditional concept of local control over the schools. We feel that this is a basic element in our educational heritage, and we certainly intend for this concept to continue under our committee's proposal." He went on to point out that the four areas most connected with local control — teachers, administration, curriculum, and requirements of local school districts — would not be affected by the committee proposal. He reminded the convention that under the 1870 constitution the General Assembly could, at any time in the past, have taken over complete control of the schools.

The presentation for the minority of the committee was made by Mathias, Buford, and Evans. Mathias made four points: (1) before a mandate is frozen into the constitution the effects which it will produce ought to be ascertained and, in the case of the majority proposal, possible results had not been sufficiently investigated; (2) the legislature had been increasing the state educational appropriation yearly, and eventually total state financing might be reached by this method; (3) to produce the money needed for the majority proposal, taxes would have to be greatly increased; if the dependence were on income tax, rates would have to go up to 5 percent on individuals and 9 percent on corporations; if on consumption taxes, they would have to be doubled; (4) because of increased state regulations and standards to be met under the majority proposal, a great deal of local control would be lost.

Buford addressed himself to the leveling of the standards of educational opportunities which would allegedly accrue from the majority report. The fear of the minority of the committee, Buford stated, was that all school districts would be reduced to the level of mediocrity rather than raised to greater heights. With all districts receiving the same share of a limited amount of money and prevented from raising more than 10 percent of that amount locally, many districts would receive fewer funds for educational purposes than they had previously and few districts would receive a great deal more than at present. He added, "The great American experiment of a dynamic locally controlled free public school system will be gone. This, my dear friends, is the one institution most unique to the American way of life — the American philosophy of challenging each of us to do his best."

Evans declared that the most important reason such a proposal should not be in the constitution is that "it does freeze in a pattern that will make it very difficult for our proposed state board and the General Assembly to work in order to really bring about equitable financing for our public schools."

The usual period of questioning after the explanation was dispensed with, and the convention proceeded to amendments of the majority proposal. The first amendment was offered by Clyde Parker:

> To meet the goals of section 1 of this article the General Assembly shall raise and distribute revenue from sources other than ad valorem property taxes to the extent of 90 percent of the average total cost of public education as determined by the State Board of Education. Funds shall be distributed to the public school districts on a per-pupil basis as determined by average daily enrollment.
>
> Local school districts shall have the authority to conduct referendums to levy taxes to make up the difference to 100 percent

of their total necessary financial budget. Not more than one referendum shall be held each twelve months' period.

The purpose of this amendment was to insure that the property tax would not be further burdened, that the total cost of education, including capital outlays and debt retirement rather than just operational costs, would be considered, and most importantly that local districts could raise as much additional money beyond that provided by the state as they felt was needed.

Speaking against the amendment, Kamin said that since it was not possible to mandate the General Assembly to provide money, the amendment did not put sufficient political pressure on that body to force them to do so:

> This gives the General Assembly an escape hatch in two ways. One, the state board of education can set a low figure as being the average total cost, because there is no actual cost averaging going on. This is something merely derived by the board of education.
>
> Secondly, so long as the local districts have the authority to, by referendum, raise whatever they want at the local level, no matter how much they get from the General Assembly, you are going to continue to have the enormous disparities whereby the local districts which are wealthy can add sufficient to whatever they are getting from the General Assembly to have a much higher level of education than the poorer districts in the state.

Kamin also pointed out that there was nothing in the majority report which would require that every school district should receive the same amount of money, for the state board and the General Assembly could determine if some districts needed more. The amendment failed by a hand count of fifty-five to twenty-six.

The second of three amendments was presented by Bottino:

> The General Assembly shall be responsible for the funding of public educational institutions and services. Distribution of state funds shall provide for substantial parity of educational opportunity throughout the state, except that the General Assembly may provide additional funds for special services. The funds obtained through local taxation by or for a school district or municipality for a free school purpose shall not exceed 50 percent of

the total funds for such purpose. Full implementation date is July 1, 1976. This section is recommended for separate submission.

The main thrust of this amendment was that local districts would be allowed to provide up to 50 percent of the total cost of education. In defense of his amendment, Bottino remarked that it had been predicted that by 1980, 25 to 30 percent of the support of local schools would come from federal sources. Therefore, to freeze the 90 percent state and 10 percent local figures into the constitution as the majority report provided would be a mistake.

In speaking against the Bottino amendment Kamin pointed out that the reference to a substantial parity of educational opportunity would be likely to bring a court case in challenge of the educational system, a challenge which might be very dangerous. If the system were not adjudged to provide substantial parity, the court would have little recourse other than to void the entire system until a better one was created. He added that since the majority report referred only to operational costs, the local districts would still be supplying building costs, which compose 15 to 20 percent of the school budget. Thus, the majority proposal would let the local school districts provide about 25 to 30 percent of the total costs of education — a result not greatly different from the 50 percent provided for in the Bottino amendment. Kamin stressed that "the broader the money-raising opportunities at the local level, the wider are going to be the disparities." The amendment failed by a hand vote of fifty-one to thirty-seven.

By far the most lengthy and heated debate was over the third amendment, presented by committee chairman Mathias, which asked for the deletion of the majority proposal. It was Mathias's position that the majority proposal was unnecessary or harmful because, as he had stated earlier, the legislature had continued to increase state support; too much money would be required, causing an enormous increase in taxes; the proposal would cause a leveling and decrease in educational excellence; and local control would be destroyed or significantly reduced.

The debate on both sides of the issue centered on two factors: taxes and equal educational opportunity. Those favoring deletion of the majority proposal pointed to the great increase in taxes which the proposal would require, although virtually every delegate stated support for equal educational opportunity and increased state funds for education. These same delegates called this a legislative matter and said the legislature should be trusted since it had been gradually increasing state support. Two other points were stressed by many delegates — the lack of flexibility provided by this proposal and the fact that educational needs of all school districts are not identical.

The main emphases of those favoring the majority report were the chance it afforded for equal educational opportunity and the relief it would provide from property taxes. It was also noted that with the likely passage in November of 1970 of a referendum eliminating the personal property tax, two-thirds of which went for educational purposes, the schools would be in a difficult financial position. To these objections and others from many delegates the majority answered that the proposal did not lock in any formula, but was instead a provision that the General Assembly be responsible for the raising and distributing of 90 percent of the money for educational purposes.

The vote on the amendment was lengthy, in that twenty delegates asked to explain their vote. Again, it would appear that various delegates did not want to seem to vote "against" education as they later indicated in interviews. Many who voted in favor of the amendment to delete prefaced their vote with the word "reluctantly." The motion to delete carried by a vote of sixty-nine to thirty-eight. All but nine Democrats opposed deletion of the proposal. Only two of the nine Democrats who favored deletion were from Chicago — Leonard Foster, the black who almost never voted with the other blacks, and Louis Marolda, who should probably not be considered a Democrat since he always followed the lead of the maverick Father Lawlor.

Also in opposition to the financing suggestion, hence in favor of deletion, were most Republicans; but five of them favored the inclusion of such a statement in the constitution. These five were Howard, a member of the Young Turk faction of the Education Committee, Helen Kinney who, as has been mentioned, often voted with the Democrats, John Alexander, a young and liberal Republican, and James Thompson and Harlan Rigney, downstate Republicans who stated that they hoped that such a proposal would help rural schools in their districts.

Of the nine Independents, six voted for deletion of the financing proposal whereas three favored retention. That the measure did not receive more solid support from this group is somewhat surprising, since it was a proposal supported throughout the country almost exclusively by very liberal organizations and individuals. However, the Independents interviewed who opposed the suggestion indicated they felt the proposal had not been fully enough researched to merit inclusion in a constitution.

Only Foster of the black delegates voted against the 90 percent state financing proposal; and it was rumored among the blacks that the Democrats did not really support the majority proposal but, knowing it would fail, voted for it to placate black Democrats already somewhat dissatisfied with Democratic positions on other issues. Another rumor, as explained to the author by a confidential source, saw the Democrats hoping that the finance measure would pass so they could offer to change their votes at a later time if the Republicans would give in on some other issues of importance to the Democrats, such as home rule. Whether there was any basis to these rumors is unclear. They were denied by all Democrats interviewed.

If the rumors are disregarded, it can be seen that on the issue of school financing geography played a significant role; those delegates from the city and from some rural districts with poor schools tended to support such a drastic increase in state financing, whereas those from wealthier districts regardless of party affiliation opposed the measure, fearing the results it might have for the schools in their area.

This issue caused much controversy both inside and outside of the convention. Many newspapers in the state, including all four major Chicago papers, wrote editorials against the proposal. Many of these editorials were distributed to the delegates, so they were obviously cognizant of the disapproval of the news media. The *Chicago Tribune* editorialized:

We doubt ... that the Con-Con education committee has offered a practical proposal, and we doubt furthermore that any plan of school financing should be frozen into a state constitution. . . .

Financing of schools is a problem for the legislature, not the convention. The committee's proposal should be junked.[5]

Delegates had discussed the majority proposal with their constituents who, in general, had displayed great displeasure with it. But in this case in addition to wishing to pacify the voters, delegates responded in interviews that they were fearful of mandating in the constitution a program which they felt had not been sufficiently investigated. However, the fact that most did not want to appear to be against education was demonstrated in that almost all delegates were careful to point out their support for equal education and increased state funds.

Some members of the majority who had presented the proposal were relieved that it failed to pass.[6] These members did accomplish a significant purpose in presenting their proposal, nevertheless; conditions in the schools were described, and because of the radical nature of the proposal and the attention received from the press, the issue was brought to the public. The sponsors were hopeful they might have stimulated awareness and further thinking on the subject.

Speculation is possible about whether the outcome of this section would have been any different had the proposal included a provision for the gradual implementation of 90 percent state financing. That this was the intention of the majority was mentioned in the report which accompanied the proposal, but for reasons of constitutional purity — that is, because implementation was a matter for the schedule, not the body, of the constitution — it was not a part of the proposal itself nor was it emphasized to any extent in the debates at the full convention.

THE IMPACT OF FIRST READING

At the end of first reading remarkably little had been amended in the proposal of the Committee on Education. "The paramount" goal had been changed to "a fundamental"; the word "selected" had

[5] *Chicago Tribune,* August 1, 1970.

[6] Such a position was expressed by Dove and Kamin, for the same reasons that motivated them in committee. See Chapter III, *supra.*

been revised to read "elected or selected"; the section on financing had been deleted. Compared to other committee reports that had come before the full convention, these changes were very few. Education had undoubtedly benefited from its generally low visibility both before and during the convention: outside pressures were few, and even at the convention, only the Welfare Council of Metropolitan Chicago and the Chamber of Commerce turned serious lobbying efforts toward education. Supporters of a strong education article were not forced to "trade off" desired changes against improvements in other articles, as was at times the case in negotiations at the convention. The members of the committee were proud and elated.

The education article was revised after first reading by the Committee on Style, Drafting, and Submission. The nature of most of these changes was not substantive. However, it was unclear to Style and Drafting what was meant by the words "The Board shall establish goals, determine policies, provide for planning and evaluating educational programs, recommend financing" in section 2 of the Education Committee proposal. They wanted to know if, by these words, the state board of education would have certain powers apart from the legislature. Despite vehement objections by Clyde Parker, who wanted the board to be independent of the General Assembly, the majority of the committee stated that giving independent powers to the board would create a "fourth branch of government" and that such was not their intent. This was the only matter discussed by the committee between first and second readings.

VIII

The Education Article
at Second and Third Readings

Second reading of the education article occurred on August 13. At this time the Committee on Style, Drafting, and Submission presented the article as revised. (Italicized words are additions to the article as it stood after first reading; lined-out words indicate omissions):

Section 1. Goal — Free Schools

A fundamental goal of the People of the State ~~shall be~~ *is* the educational development of all persons to the limits of their capacities.

~~To achieve this goal, it shall be the duty of the State to~~ The State *shall* provide for an efficient system of high quality public educational institutions and services.

Education in ~~the~~ public schools through the secondary level shall be free. There may be such other free education as the General Assembly provides *by law*.

Section 2. State Board of Education — Chief State Educational Officer

There ~~shall be~~ *is created* a State Board of Education *to be* elected or ~~selected~~ *appointed* on a regional basis. The number of members, their qualifications, terms of office and manner of selection shall be provided by law. The Board shall establish goals, determine policies, provide for planning and evaluating

education programs, recommend financing and have such jurisdiction, *duties and* powers ~~and duties~~ as provided by law.

~~There shall be a chief educational officer appointed by~~ The
State Board of Education *shall appoint a chief state educational
officer.*

Section 3. Public Funds for Sectarian Purposes Forbidden

Neither the General Assembly nor any county, city, town, township, school district, or other public corporation, shall ever make
any appropriation or pay from any public fund whatever, anything in aid of any church or sectarian purpose, or to help support or sustain any school, academy, seminary, college, university,
or other literary or scientific institution, controlled by any church
or sectarian denomination whatever; nor shall any grant or donation of land, money, or other personal property ever be made by
the State, or any such public corporation, to any church, or for
any sectarian purpose.

After approval of an amendment changing section 2 to read
"elected or selected" rather than "appointed," and "election or
selection" rather than "selection" (thus restoring the language as
it had been after first reading), the report of the Committee on
Style, Drafting, and Submission was accepted.

The next amendment submitted at second reading was from
Parker, who tried to make the section coincide with his interpretation. His amendment stipulated.

The Board shall establish goals, determine policies, provide for
planning and evaluating education programs and recommend
financing. The Board shall have such other jurisdiction, duties
and powers as provided by law.

The amendment was submitted jointly with Pughsley, who also felt
that the board should be independent of the legislature in such
areas as establishing goals and policies; it was thus they argued to
the full convention.

Mathias contended that the board should not have independent
powers and moved a substitution which read:

The Board, except as limited by law, may establish goals, determine policies, provide for planning and evaluating education programs, and recommend financing. The Board shall have such other
duties and powers as provided by law.

In explaining this new wording Mathias stated:

> Under this language as proposed in this substitute amendment,
> the board would have certain authority and powers and could
> go ahead, but if the legislature is not in agreement with what
> they have done, then the legislature would establish different
> policies and different planning and evaluation programs and so
> on. The board would not have powers that the General Assembly would not override and not abrogate.

The Mathias substitution for the Parker amendment was adopted without significant debate by a hand vote of fifty-two to nine.

Henry Green, a Republican from Urbana, offered an amendment which dealt further with this question. In effect, it proposed to make all activities of the state board initiate from the General Assembly, rather than allowing the board to go ahead until vetoed or restrained by the legislature:

> The Board shall have such jurisdiction, powers, and duties as
> provided by law.

Green, perhaps speaking for the representatives of higher education, offered his amendment mainly out of a fear that the Mathias amendment would create a superboard over all of education. It was pointed out, however, that the board could well become functionless under the Green amendment unless duties were provided by the General Assembly. The members of the Education Committee also emphasized that the Mathias amendment was not meant to create a superboard, although it contained the flexibility to allow that. The Green amendment failed by a hand vote of sixty to fourteen.

Dwight Friedrich, a Republican from Centralia, proposed an amendment similar to one that had been offered at first reading. It stated:

> A chief state educational officer may be appointed by the State
> Board of Education or he may be selected as otherwise provided
> by law.

The amendment failed on a voice vote without significant debate. Another suggestion, by Robert Butler, Republican from Marion, would have made the state board an elected body; this amendment was also defeated with little discussion, by a voice vote of forty-eight to thirty-seven.

The last proposed amendment to section 2 was offered by Chicago Democrat Paul Elward and added after the word "basis" in the committee proposal:

> provided that any such board shall be elected or selected so as to give substantially equal representation to all people in the State.

It was noted in the debate that the proposal accepted on first reading provided for election or selection "on a regional basis," which would mean districts subject to the one man–one vote rule if board members were elected. If appointed, they would still have to be selected on a regional basis, but it would be very difficult to have equal representation by population. This amendment also failed, with little debate, by a hand count of forty-one to twenty-seven. It may have been that Elward — like most Chicago Democrats, in favor of the election of state officials — was trying to make the elective method more likely to be the choice of the General Assembly.

The wording of section 2 after second reading was, therefore:

> There is created a State Board of Education to be elected or selected on a regional basis. The number of members, their qualifications, terms of office and manner of election or selection shall be provided by law. The Board, except as limited by law, may establish goals, determine policies, provide for planning and evaluating education programs and recommend financing. The Board shall have such other duties and powers as provided by law.
>
> The State Board of Education shall appoint a chief state educational officer.

Two amendments were offered at second reading to section 3, on aid to nonpublic schools. The first, proposed by Father Lawlor, stated:

> Nothing contained in this article shall be construed to deny children the right to pray or receive religious instruction in private religiously oriented schools which are State chartered and conform to standards and requirements of the Illinois School Code.

In explaining his amendment Father Lawlor stated:

The Supreme Court has approved various forms of financial aid, forms of bus transportation, school lunch programs, and so forth; and if such programs are extended by law to parochial schools, I don't want to see the children gradually placed in the posture where the continuance of such financial aid will be cause for denying them their right to pray or to receive religious instruction in their own private schools.

The Education Committee pointed out that there was nothing in their article that would deny the right to pray in private schools. A roll call was requested on the amendment, and sixteen delegates asked to explain their votes. Many voted no because they did not know what the full implications of the amendment would be; others stated that nothing in the article would deny the right to pray in private schools — that the amendment was referring to an interference that did not exist. The proposal failed by a roll call vote of fifty-four to forty-one with six passing.

No Independent voted in favor of the Lawlor proposal; sixteen Republicans supported it, and twenty-two Democrats. Of those Democrats in favor of the amendment nineteen were Catholics. In their interviews delegates indicated confusion as to the meaning of this amendment, but all stated that private schools should be allowed to provide whatever religious instruction they wished.

The second amendment on this topic moved to delete section 3 entirely. The debate on the proposal, offered by Harold Nudelman, a Chicago Democrat, was a reiteration of statements made at first reading, and after only three speakers it was moved that the debate be closed. The vote was forty-three in favor of the amendment and fifty-nine against it; one delegate passed. Only one Independent, Peter Tomei, a Catholic, voted for the amendment. All but ten Republicans — four of them Catholics — opposed the proposal, whereas only eleven Democrats were against. None of these eleven were white Chicago Democrats and none of them were Catholics. At first reading all but one black delegate had voted against removal of section 3, but at second reading three of the blacks from Chicago — Kemp, Coleman, and Nicholson — appeared to succumb to the pressure of the Chicago Democratic organization and voted in favor of deletion of the section. Many other Catholics were willing to follow the recommendation of the Illinois Catholic Conference to leave the section unchanged. Therefore, although this cannot be seen as a completely Catholic versus non-Catholic issue, delegates from within and without the Chicago Democratic organization have assured the author that the largely Catholic Chicago Democratic organization was applying pressure on its delegates to attain some measure favorable to, or at least not contrary to, aid to nonpublic schools. With the failure of the Nudelman amendment, section 3 remained unchanged after second reading.

The amendments to the education article to which the convention gave the closest attention at second reading were the two which dealt with the financing of the public school system. The first amendment, offered by Dawn Clark Netsch, an Independent from Chicago's twelfth district, proposed a new section 4:

> The state has the primary responsibility for financing the system of educational institutions and services.

In explaining her amendment Netsch admitted it was hortatory language not legally enforceable. However, she continued:

> I do believe that it serves two purposes. One, while it is not legally enforceable, I hope that it will function as a conscience to the General Assembly to assume a greater proportion of the financing of the public schools of the state.
>
> Secondly, I have been impressed in this Convention with a very widespread sentiment among the delegates that the state should assume a much greater proportion of the burden of financing of public schools. If I am right that that is, indeed, a widespread sentiment, it seems to me that it would be unfortunate for this constitution, which does express basic commitments on the part of the state, not to express it in some form or another.

The second amendment, offered by Bottino as a substitute for the Netsch amendment, read:

> The General Assembly shall be responsible for the funding of public educational institutions and services. Distribution of State funds shall provide for a substantial parity of educational opportunity throughout the State, except that the General Assembly may provide additional funds for special services.

> The funds obtained through local taxation by or for a school district or municipality for a free school purpose shall not exceed 50 percent of the total funds for such purposes.
>
> Full implementation date, July 1, 1976. Recommended for separate submission.

Bottino explained that, unlike the Netsch amendment, his language was not hortatory and did not leave to the General Assembly a duty about which they had been lax in the past.

The main debate on the Netsch amendment centered on whether the word "primary" meant the state should have the largest share in financing the public schools or whether it meant it was the state's first obligation to finance the public schools. Netsch intended the former. Speaking for the majority of the committee, Dove stated they would favor Bottino's amendment and — if that failed — Netsch's, because both amendments addressed themselves to increased state support. Kamin, however, said the Bottino amendment did not go far enough and the Netsch amendment did not go anywhere. The Bottino amendment failed by a voice vote and the Netsch amendment failed by a hand vote of forty-seven to thirty-eight.

With the exception of one successful amendment intended to clarify the meaning of section 2 and the two amendments on financing which failed, almost all other changes suggested at second reading were merely reiterations of points that had been disposed of at first reading. Those with biases for election of state officials and those hoping for more aid to nonpublic schools were the most persistent in attempting to have their interests included in the constitution. They failed, however, because the majority of the delegates apparently did not want to freeze a system of selection into the state charter when it dealt with education, nor did they want to arouse a controversy which might endanger the ratification of the document.

The vote to send the education article after second reading to Style and Drafting was not unanimous. Some delegates voted against it because of the "religious bigotry" contained in section 3, whereas others agreed with Pughsley, who said, "I vote no, because I do not feel the education article, the committee nor the Convention, addressed itself to the serious educational problems of the state of Illinois." She explained in an interview that, in her opinion, the state board of education should have been given independent powers and that the state should have taken over the financing of the public schools. She felt that had she not been ill for so long, she might have been able to help the committee create a better article.

Other delegates gave specific reasons for voting against the article: Father Lawlor felt it perpetuated bigotry; Rosewell and Elward agreed with Pughsley. It is likely, however, that Rosewell and Elward, Catholic delegates like almost all others who voted against the article, were objecting more to the retention of section 3 than to the lack of independent powers of the state board or the failure of the passage of a system of increased funding from the state level. An analysis of the roll call vote shows that of the fifteen delegates voting against approving the education article, all but two were Democrats. Of the two non-Democrats, one was Father Lawlor, whose objections have been mentioned above, and the other was James Thompson, a downstate Republican, who felt that the convention should have made some provisions for increased state financing. The pass votes were made by Lawlor's follower Marolda and Ray Garrison, a conservative Republican who considered section 1 of the education article too broadly stated. The article was approved, however, by a vote of eighty-four to fifteen with two passes.

THIRD READING

At third reading it was necessary to suspend the rules by a two-thirds vote to debate or vote on any substantive amendments. An attempt to do so when the education article was considered at third reading on August 31 was made by Lawlor; he wished to consider the following amendment to section 3:

> Neither the General Assembly nor any county, city, town, township, school district or other public corporation shall ever make any appropriation or pay from any public fund whatever, anything in aid of any church for any sectarian purpose.
>
> Financial aid to support or sustain any school, academy, seminary, college, university or other literary or scientific institution controlled by any church or sectarian denomination shall be strictly limited to public purpose only.

No grant or donation of land, money or other personal property shall ever be made by the State, or any such corporation, to any church for any sectarian purpose.

Although Lawlor stated he did not consider the amendment a substantive change from the present section 3, close examination of the wording of the Lawlor proposal would indicate that it was a very large change in the intent of the section in that, in emphasizing "sectarian purpose" and "public purpose only," it would have made plans for state financial support for teaching of secular subjects in private schools easier to accomplish. It was ruled to be substantive, hence to require suspension of the rules. The proposal did not receive the necessary two-thirds vote to open debate since the final tally was forty-six to forty-six with five passes.

Of the Republicans, only eleven voted in favor of opening debate on the issue; eight of these eleven were Catholics. All but two of the Independents voted against allowing debate. Tomei favored further discussion, and Ronald Smith, another Independent Catholic, passed. Only eight Democrats voted against opening discussion on the issue and of these all but Kamin, Patch, and the unpredictable black delegate Leonard Foster were from Downstate rather than Chicago. Either the Chicago Democratic organization was applying even stronger pressure at this time, or many delegates felt they could vote for opening debate and then vote against the amendment, for all black delegates but Patch and Foster voted to allow discussion. This was quite a change from first reading, when all but one black delegate voted against amendment of section 3.

By a vote of seventy to twenty-nine, however, with three passes, the convention did allow reconsideration of the Netsch amendment which had been defeated at second reading. The amendment stated, in revised form,

The State has the primary responsibility for financing the system of public educational institutions and services.

In explaining her reasons for presenting the amendment again, Netsch said there was widespread sentiment in the convention for the state to assume a greater portion of school financing; as proof, she noted that sixty-eight people had signed her amendment as cosponsors. She again pointed out the statement was not legally enforceable but did indicate the direction in which the convention wished the legislature to move.

Most debate was not on this amendment per se but rather on a substitute presented by Kamin, Dove, Fogal, and Howard which stipulated:

> The state shall undertake to provide substantially all funds for the financing of the free public schools from revenues other than real property taxes.

Speaking for the sponsors of the amendment Kamin stated that although they had previously favored the Netsch amendment, they had begun to feel that it really accomplished very little. Kamin claimed to have discovered, when talking to the sponsors of the Netsch proposal, that all held varying ideas as to just what the language was meant to do. Since the purpose in general was to achieve greater equality of education while relieving the property tax burden, Kamin felt the substitute amendment was more clearly expressed and more directly to the purpose. He pointed out that the substitute was also a hortatory statement, perhaps more so than the Netsch amendment. He felt Netsch's amendment could allow dangerous suits to the effect that property taxes were too great, since the state had not yet undertaken the primary responsibility for financing the school system. Rather than increasing money spent on education, the Netsch amendment could, Kamin felt, mean a decrease in education at the local level without a concomitant increase at the state level. This was so because local taxpayers might refuse to support education at any level which meant a greater-than-50 percent contribution from local, as opposed to state, taxes. A judicial decision would then be required to determine the meaning of "primary." Kamin's amendment was an attempt to put pressure on the state as opposed to the local school districts, and to force a political, rather than a judicial, decision.[1]

The most vehement opposition to this substitution came from Mathias and Albert Raby, a Chicago black Independent. Mathias emphasized that the amendment could be interpreted even more

---

[1] Kamin was apparently correct. See *Blase* v. *State*, 55 Ill. 2d 94, 302 N.E. 2d 46 (1973), and the discussion of school financing in Chapter IX, *infra*.

broadly than the majority proposal defeated at first reading. He also reiterated arguments dealing with loss of local control, lowering of educational standards, and the undetermined effects that might accrue from such a proposal. Raby's opposition was very surprising, since he had been one of the convention's strongest advocates of full state financing. Although he purportedly objected to the substitute amendment because it was merely hortatory in nature and declared: "I think people are playing games," Raby had other objections he privately admitted later. He realized that the Netsch amendment also was hortatory, so this was not the source of his main objection. In fact, he voted against the substitution because its sponsors had failed to consult Pughsley. Not knowing of the existence of the substitute to be proposed by some members of her committee, Pughsley signed the Netsch amendment, thus indicating that she was a cosponsor. This placed her in a somewhat awkward position, since she greatly favored increased state support, which might better have been provided by the substitute amendment. Therefore, Raby was not objecting to the substitute itself, the subject matter of which he favored, but to the way in which it had been handled.[2] After he, as a leader of the liberal, Independent forces, stated his opposition, the substitute had no chance for passage and was defeated by a hand vote of fifty-eight to thirty. The Netsch amendment, however, with little debate, passed, also by a hand vote, sixty-five to twenty-eight. The education article was then sent to Style and Drafting for enrollment into the proposed constitution.

Although the votes on the Netsch amendment and on the substitute were hand votes and do not permit analysis, some idea of delegate positions on this issue may be gained from an examination of the roll call vote on whether debate should be allowed on the subject of school financing. As previously mentioned, the vote to allow debate was seventy to twenty-nine with three passes. All Independents and all blacks voted to allow reconsideration of the amendment. Only five Democrats voted against reconsideration, but since four of these were Chicago Democrats it would appear that this was not a party issue. The three pass votes were registered by Law-

[2] Albert Raby, in an interview with the author, August 31, 1970.

lor and by downstate Republicans Martin and Ozinga. Marolda voted in opposition to reconsideration, but the remaining opposition came from Republicans, the majority of whom were from suburban or downstate districts with fine school systems. Again it would appear that on the issue of financing of the public schools geography was the most important criterion.

The final vote to approve the education article at third reading, as at second reading, was not unanimous. The tally was eighty-nine in favor, ten opposed, and two passing. The two who passed, Garrison and Friedrich, were conservative Republicans who had also voted against reconsideration of the Netsch amendment. Of the ten who voted against approval, five were other conservative Republicans who had also voted against reconsideration of the Netsch amendment. Of the remaining five, one was Marolda, who objected to section 3 because of the ban on aid to nonpublic schools; Lawlor was not present for the vote but it can be assumed he would have voted with Marolda. The other four negative votes were all Catholic Democrats, presumably with the same objections as Marolda.

After third reading Style and Drafting made a minor revision in the new finance section added to section 1 of the education article. The final version read: "The State has the primary responsibility for financing the system of public education," rather than "the system of public educational institutions and services," as originally written by Netsch. There were no other changes from the text of the article after second reading. The final education article as it was to be submitted to the people of Illinois read:

Article X. Education

Section 1. Goal — Free Schools

A fundamental goal of the People of the State is the educational development of all persons to the limits of their capacities.

The State shall provide for an efficient system of high quality public educational institutions and services. Education in public schools through the secondary level shall be free. There may be such other free education as the General Assembly provides by law.

The State has the primary responsibility for financing the system of public education.

Section 2. State Board of Education — Chief State Educational
    Officer

(a) There is created a State Board of Education to be elected
or selected on a regional basis. The number of members, their
qualifications, terms of office and manner of election or selection
shall be provided by law. The Board, except as limited by law,
may establish goals, determine policies, provide for planning and
evaluating education programs and recommend financing. The
Board shall have such other duties and powers as provided by
law.

(b) The State Board of Education shall appoint a chief state
educational officer.

Section 3. Public Funds for Sectarian Purposes Forbidden

Neither the General Assembly nor any county, city, town, township, school district, or other public corporation, shall ever make
any appropriation or pay from any public fund whatever, anything in aid of any church or sectarian purpose, or to help support
or sustain any school, academy, seminary, college, university, or
other literary or scientific institution, controlled by any church or
sectarian denomination whatever; nor shall any grant or donation
of land, money, or other personal property ever be made by the
State, or any such public corporation, to any church, or for any
sectarian purpose.

It is interesting that, as it turned out, the full convention tended
to react to each educational issue in the same manner as the majority on the Education Committee had reacted. Where there had
been complete agreement in the committee, such as in the section
dealing with the state board of education, there was virtually no significant change from the committee proposal at the full convention.
Where there had been some doubts raised, as in section 1, the convention also expressed doubts and somewhat altered the wording.
Where there was dissension, as over finance, there was too much
dissension in the convention to facilitate passage of a strong measure. Where there was fear, as in section 3, fear was expressed in
the full convention, and the section was left unchanged.

The committee had demonstrated its skill in assessing just how
much could be passed by the full convention, which in turn was
successful in its assessment of passage by the voters. In the two areas

of doubt in the committee — the use of the words "the paramount" and the section on finance — the committee rightly judged that pushing for strong language would result in a more desirable compromise at the full convention. All members of the committee expressed pleasure at the final outcome of their article — an article which, with the exception of section 3, is simple and concise and yet perhaps expresses the strongest commitment to education among the fifty states.

Like the actions of the Education Committee, those of the full convention can best be interpreted by the concept of a conflict over the degree of change to be incorporated into the education article. The full convention was unwilling to accept any provision of too radical a nature; thus they rejected the words "the paramount" in section 1 and the section on total state financing because they wished to placate the voters. This desire for pacification of the people was also the consideration that decided the outcome of the section on aid to nonpublic schools despite the pressure applied by the Chicago Democratic organization. In addition, the "nonpolitical" nature of education, as shown by the lack of party or bloc voting in many educational areas at the convention and as indicated by the delegates in interviews, helped to keep the delegates from making further changes in the innovative nature of the article.

The full convention allowed the Education Committee to take the lead on its article, unlike other committees which dealt with more political subjects, and no delegate who was not on the Education Committee was particularly influential in educational matters at the full convention. However, the Chicago Democratic organization may be seen as an important influence on the issue of aid to nonpublic schools. The fact that the convention looked to the committee (or to part of the committee, as in the finance section) as the experts on education — except perhaps for the Chicago Catholics, who took their lead from the Democratic organization in their position on aid to nonpublic schools — the fact that no one wished to seem to vote against education, and the fact that the education article as reported from committee was of an innovative nature allowed the final article to retain much of its original strength after the convention had completed its debates on the subject.

IX

Conclusions and Implications

With the ratification of the new constitution by the voters in December of 1970, Illinois obtained a new education article. That article was not a significant factor in the passage of the entire document; in fact, relatively little attention was given to education by the press or by individuals or groups working for or against passage of the proposed constitution. However, it is possible to speculate that the 1970 education article may promote the most far-reaching changes of any article in the new document — changes in the method of financing education, in the scope of education, in the very nature of the educational process in Illinois.

Section 1 of the article provides almost limitless possibilities for increasing the scope of education, by calling for the education of all people to "the limits of their capacities." This goal, when taken with the sentence "Education in public schools through the secondary level shall be free" can be interpreted to mean that adults as well as those under twenty-one must receive education through the high school level at no charge — a concept of educational responsibility unique in this country.[1] If the same reasoning holds true, the article

[1] It is possible that the constitutions of Indiana and Georgia could be interpreted in this light. Indiana provides in Article VIII, section 1, for a system of "Common Schools, wherein tuition shall be without charge, and equally open to all." Georgia states in Article VIII, section 1: "The provision of an adequate education for the citizens shall be a primary obligation of the State of Georgia, the expense of which shall be provided for by taxation." However, in Indiana it is not likely that this section, written in 1851, was intended to apply to adults, especially since it uses the term "Common Schools." In Georgia, the term "adequate" might be seen as applying to much less than education through the secondary level.

apparently also requires that the physically and mentally handi-capped be guaranteed an education to the limits of their capacities.

As mentioned in Chapter III, section 1 is being interpreted broadly by some to include areas not previously considered to be part of the educational system: One organization has called the new constitution "an expression of the State's obligation to support the arts beyond their inclusion in formal educational program, to provide cultural opportunities to 'all persons to the limits of their capacities.' "[2] Researchers at the University of Chicago law and education schools have been federally funded to investigate ways of holding school systems legally accountable for failure to provide students with a minimum education. Any suit to that effect in Illi-nois would probably be brought on the basis of the phrase "to the limits of their capacities."[3]

It was predicted at the convention that the sentence in section 1, "The State has the primary responsibility for financing the system of public education," would be a subject for legal challenge. By September of 1973, the Illinois Supreme Court had already handed down its first interpretation of that sentence. In *Blase* v. *State*,[4] the plaintiffs had sued to force the state to provide at least 50 percent of the funds for Illinois's public school system, basing their suit on the word "primary" in section 1 of the education article. Relying on the transcripts of the 1970 convention, the court held that the sentence on financing was merely hortatory — "that the sentence was in-tended only to express a goal or objective, and not to state a specific command."[5]

Yet, especially since 1971, the issue of school financing has be-come one of the most controversial in the educational arena. In *San Antonio Independent School District* v. *Rodriguez*[6] it was held that Texas did not violate the Fourteenth Amendment to the federal Constitution by basing its school finance system upon local property

[2] Illinois, Advisory Commission on Financing the Arts in Illinois, *Report* (Chicago, 1971), p. 4.

[3] In a recent article, Stephen Sugarman of the University of California Law School described the progress of a suit against the San Francisco public schools on the basis of similar language. *School Review* 82 (February 1974): 233–59.

[4] 55 Ill.2d 94, 302 N.E.2d 46, 1973.

[5] Ibid., p. 98.

[6] 411 U.S. 1 (1973).

taxes from districts of unequal wealth. This case is in direct contradiction to the now famous *Serrano* v. *Priest*[7] decision of the California Supreme Court, which in 1971 held the California school finance system to be unconstitutional because it *did* discriminate against the people in those districts with a poor tax base. While *Rodriguez* would seem to settle the issue of whether state school financing systems violate the federal equal protection clause, it does not preclude challenges on the state level. For example, *Serrano* is considered to have been decided on the basis of the California equal protection clause, and is thus apparently still binding within that state despite *Rodriguez*. In 1972, the Michigan Supreme Court relied on its own state constitution to reach a decision similar to *Serrano* in the case of *Governor* v. *State Treasurer*.[8] Property tax systems for the financing of public schools have also been struck down by state courts on grounds other than equal protection. For example, a New Jersey court declared that state's school financing system unconstitutional because it did not meet the requirement of a "thorough and efficient" school system in the New Jersey Constitution.[9]

Delegate Malcolm Kamin has recently speculated, however, that the school financing language in the Illinois Constitution may be an impediment to court reform of educational finance:

> If the Illinois school financing system is further challenged in the courts, the new equal protection clause in the Illinois Bill of Rights, together with the 'efficient system' language of the Educational Article, should compel a *Serrano*-like result. Such a result could fail to materialize solely because an Illinois court reasons that the convention, having addressed itself to school finance in the last sentence of section 1 of article X, did not intend any other provisions of the new constitution to control school financing. That would be a strong blow to the advocates of equal educational opportunity [since the sentence in section one has been

[7] 5 Cal.3d 584, 487 P.2d 1241, 96 Cal. Rptr. 601 (1971).

[8] 389 Mich. 1, 203 N.W.2d 457 (1972).

[9] *Robinson* v. *Cahill*, 62 N.J. 473, 303 A.2d 273 (1973). Illinois's phrase, "The State shall provide for an efficient system of high quality public educational institutions and services," is in the same vein and may be the basis of a similar challenge.

termed merely hortatory]. Yet, such reasoning is not beyond the range of possibility.[10]

Kamin continues:

> Hopefully, such a case will not be necessary. If the legislature and the new State Board of Education will take the school financing language for what it is — the statement of a pressing problem and the urgent prayer for a fair solution — then they will act to equalize educational opportunity and the tax burdens of educational financing without further judicial intervention.[11]

The action (or non-action) taken by the convention which proved most significant in securing passage of the constitution may have been its decision to leave section 3 on aid to nonpublic schools unchanged. Experts testifying to the Education Committee, as well as most of the members themselves, came to the conclusion that the United States Supreme Court — in the light of such decisions as *Allen*[12] — would be likely to interpret the Illinois ban more loosely than would appear warranted on its face. Thus were advocates of more aid to nonpublic schools placated at the convention by the retention of section 3, whereas opponents of aid, who recognized the difficulty of creating stronger language, hoped the section would be strictly interpreted. Had the convention changed section 3, by making it either weaker or stronger, the heated controversy necessarily engendered might have proven detrimental to the passage of the entire constitution: this was the one educational issue on which emotions were high and interest group pressure could have been strong.

Moreover, any controversy engendered by an attempt to loosen the ban would apparently have been futile, for in 1971 the United States Supreme Court, in *Lemon* v. *Kurtzman*,[13] seemed to provide a definitive "no" to questions of aiding nonpublic schools. The decision — which apparently bars even parental vouchers and systems designed to reimburse teachers of secular subjects in nonpublic

[10] "The School Finance Language of the Education Article: The Chimerical Mandate," *John Marshall Journal of Practice and Procedure* 6 (Spring, 1973): 331.

[11] Ibid., p. 345.

[12] *Board of Education* v. *Allen*, 392 U.S. 236 (1968). See Chapter V, *supra*.

[13] 403 U.S. 602 (1971).

schools — was unexpected. Most experts thought the interpretation of the court would be more liberal. In fact, the 1971 Illinois legislature had passed a bill allowing certain kinds of aid for nonpublic schools. However, after *Lemon*, all such attempts seem futile.[14] Thus, in taking no action on the question, the convention avoided what might have been a needless defeat of the whole document.

THE POLITICS OF EDUCATION

That there exists an intimate relationship between education and politics was unthinkable until recently. Politics to most people conjures up images of wheeling and dealing, of under-the-table payoffs, of patronage, spoils, and flamboyant oratory with no substance. Educators struggled to keep education untainted by anything political: the public schools as the bastion of democracy had to remain "above" politics; education was described as a unique function of government which merited special treatment.

Gradually this attitude has become eroded. Professional educators as well as the general public have realized that since more public money is spent for education than for any other single function of state and local governments, decision making on this subject is of necessity going to be political — a reflection of competition and compromise between various interest groups and power factions. And yet, at the constitutional convention one still heard such comments as "Politics and education don't mix" and "I am not being political on this subject, but . . ." or such contradictions as "My constituents insist that politics be kept out of education but that their interests be represented."

As mentioned in Chapter I, one of the reasons given for not wanting to serve on the Education Committee at Con-Con was that it would be the least political and thus the least important of the committees. Such was not the case, either in process or in product. The Education Committee, in its day-to-day workings, was extremely political. Conflicts over reform versus the status quo gave rise to factions and to political gamesmanship. Issues were decided

[14] More recently, the United States Supreme Court struck down other plans for providing aid to nonpublic schools in *Committee for Public Education & Religious Liberty* v. *Nyquist*, 413 U.S. 756 (1973).

finally by compromise, a familiar procedure in the political process. On the issue of financing, where the committee failed to reach compromise, it was the desire of certain members not to vote with the "opponent" which permitted the presentation of full state financing to the convention; this, in turn, created a situation in which compromise was necessary among all of the delegates on the financing issue.

The decision to keep the convention open — to permit public attendance at all meetings, to make debate and votes available for scrutiny, and to involve the citizens in the convention process through public hearings — was in reality a very "politic" scheme formulated to assure passage of the charter. Because of this openness, the public became aware of the omission of the word "free" from section 1 of the education article and was able to apply pressure toward eventual compromise — a very political process. At the full convention the fact that votes were recorded and often published made the delegates, especially those with political ambitions, hesitant to risk irritating their constituents by appearing to vote against education. Thus it is likely that the resulting education article was more innovative than it would have been had delegate debate and votes not been available to the public.

The state board of education created by the convention was a political product. Its implementation by the legislature and its functions after implementation have been or will be political. The legislature took almost two years to agree on language establishing the board, debating again and again questions like those which had plagued the committee: should members be elected or appointed? If appointed, by whom and on what basis? If elected, from what regions? When they did pass a bill creating a board of seventeen members, the governor — who was given the power of appointment — had to give significant attention to balancing political party and interest group affiliation. The board itself is still all potential at this moment. But because this body will be dealing with a political subject, that of education, various questions arise as to its future: Will it become factionalized along party lines? Will it be conservative or innovative in nature? Will it lead or follow the legislature? Will it become a forum for the interest groups with power in the state? Or will it attempt to isolate itself from such segments? What will be its relationship to established local boards? Will it handle such controversial issues as the accountability of teachers, equal educational opportunity, teacher militancy, and the financing of education, or leave those questions to the local school boards? If it does attack the controversial issues, what will be its general direction in deciding them? The answers are unknown as of this writing, but the answers, like the questions, will not be apolitical.

No longer can professional educators afford to maintain that education is separate from or "above" politics, that it is educators alone who can serve the public interest in this area. Politics, in the general sense, refers to the methods by which social values and financial resources are allocated for different purposes and among different people. In Illinois various interest groups are banding together to influence these values and the allocation of these resources: parents are demanding that teachers be held accountable for what students do or do not learn; teachers are becoming militant: strikes, unheard of a decade ago, are now commonplace; the Illinois Education Association, representing many of Illinois's teachers, is endorsing political candidates and helping to finance their campaigns; students themselves are organizing to obtain rights not previously granted them. Rather than abstaining from politics, individuals and groups with a vested interest in education must instead become skilled practitioners of politics, employing all of its most useful tools, and engaging in all of its traditional practices. They must compromise, bargain, wheel and deal, and meet in lots of closed, smoke-filled rooms where the real business of education is being discussed. The creation of the education article of the new Illinois Constitution shows that education and politics can and will mix.

Index